What People Are Saying About
ON MY WATCH

This is a terrific book. Martha Johnson gives page after page of advice for new and old leaders. And that advice is useful for every leader: government, corporate, non-profit. When you come down it, leaders need to see situations clearly, imagine where to go and make the organization excited to get there. This book is a terrific manual for that.

I know Martha well. She's a good leader; she's also a good advisor, a good listener and a good follower. As you read *On My Watch*, think about the good leadership you have seen. I think you'll change some of your ideas and gain plenty of new insight.

Dave Barram,
Former Administrator, US GSA;
former executive at HP, SGI and Apple

Vintage Martha Johnson! A clear, direct and compelling expression of her extraordinary, and all too brief, leadership journey at GSA. Packed with leadership lessons for the 21st century, it is a very worthy read.

Douglas R. Conant
Former President and CEO of Campbell Soup Company,
Founder and Chairman of Kellogg Executive Leadership Institute

I congratulate Martha Johnson on her book and its obvious importance to readers who are confronting some of the same challenges of leadership that she faced.

William H. Donaldson
Founding Dean, Yale University's School of Management,
Former Chairman of the SEC

On My Watch offers us ways to think about how the too-often hidden stories of innovation in our government deserve applause, support, and further study. We will never get the government we want if all we find are the problems with it.

Max Stier,
President and CEO, Partnership for Public Service

On My Watch is almost unique among business books in telling the story of leading a huge, complex institution in human terms. Martha Johnson understands that business and government are about people, and she describes the lessons she has learned in a language too seldom seen in management texts, full of words like passion, enthusiasm, loyalty, trust, accountability and justice. Her management story is a human story, full of tragedy, hope and nobility.

David Newkirk
Former CEO-Executive Education, The University of Virginia's
Darden School of Business, and Senior Partner, Booz & Co.

In *On My Watch*, Johnson weaves together two big ideas: the extraordinary challenges and rewards of leading large government organizations and the personal risks of assuming those responsibilities. The result is sharp, open and a pleasure to read.

Nelson Ford
President and CEO, LMI

What a wonderful teaching tool. Johnson leads the students right into the core of what leadership in the public sector is really all about.This material will make a substantial contribution to the literature and education of future civil servants.

Walter Broadnax
Distinguished Professor of Public and International Affairs
at the Maxwell School of Syracuse University and formerly
Deputy Secretary of Health and Human Services

On My Watch should be a must-read book for all those in, or preparing for, public service. It provides breakthrough examples of what can be done in government agencies, even huge ones, to inspire enthusiasm, focus actions, increase efficiency, and reduce waste. If that were not enough, it also provides a powerful strategy for reaching timely decisions that involve input from all the key stakeholders—a strategy that could transform how things are done in Washington. In addition, it provides a powerful example of grace under pressure in a leader who demonstrates high integrity in times of success as well as when, through no fault of her own, she takes a big one for the team. Martha Johnson and this book are class acts of the first order.

Carol Pearson, Ph. D.
Author of *The Hero and the Outlaw: Extraordinary Branding Through the Power of Archetypes*, and former Professor of Leadership Studies in the School of Public Policy at the University of Maryland and Director of the James MacGregor Burns Academy of Leadership

Change in all organizations is an entrepreneurial endeavor requiring more than sound management. Successfully changing an organization's culture to allow for creativity, innovation, collaboration and teamwork requires strong leadership. My personal thanks to Martha Johnson for sharing her thoughts and experiences in a rare book of ideas that can help leaders of all organizations effect change.

Gerald G. Kokos
President and CEO, VFA, Inc.

Whether you lead a team of 10 or 10,000 this book will inspire you to do it better. It's not only a treasure trove of insights into what it takes to be a great leader, it's a beautifully written story of passion, innovation, determination, wisdom and humility.

Kate Lister
President of Global Workplace Analytics

You are unlikely to become the largest landlord in the universe (in this case, managing more than $500 billion in federal property), operate a fleet with hundreds of thousands of cars, and have as your clients the U.S. President and his cabinet—all as merely part of your mission to efficiently build and operate the U.S. Government's physical infrastructure. But that was Martha Johnson's job description as head of the U.S. General Services Administration. In *On My Watch,* she reveals, in a remarkably unpretentious style, both the leadership techniques that facilitated her to rise to the top and the missteps that led to her fall.

Jim Snider
2012-2013 Fellow, Edmond J. Safra Center for Ethics,
Harvard University

Martha Johnson is a leader's leader. Having told her story with grace and wit about how "life happened" to her in an excruciatingly public way, she then makes sense of it in pursuit of the holy grail of leadership: self-awareness. If you aspire to the halls of power (or the next rung on your organizational ladder) please read this book and take to heart its central theme–the facts of your life are just the facts, and much of what happens to you is out of your control; what matters most on your leadership journey, however, is always at your command... your personal narrative and how you use it to face what's next.

Harry Hutson
Leadership Coach, Co-Author *Putting Hope to Work*
and *Leadership in Non-Profit Organizations*

Leading an organization of any size requires seeing around corners–being able to predict the next event that might bring disaster or untold opportunity. *On My Watch* is a must-read for anyone who plans to lead a high-profile organization and needs to know how to lead when the unexpected inevitably happens.

Richard J. Crespin
Co-Founder *Corporate Responsibility Magazine* & CEO, Crespin Enterprises

Martha Johnson's out-of-the-box brilliance will inspire anyone who reads this book. I love her vulnerability and accessibility—she's the kind of person most people would love to have as their leader. She also gives us a glimpse of the best of government—making me wish I had continued in government service after my two years with the Peace Corps.

Jennifer Read Hawthorne
Co-author, #1 *New York Times* best seller *Chicken Soup for the Woman's Soul* and *The Soul of Success*

On My Watch

Leadership, Innovation, and
Personal Resilience

ON MY WATCH

Leadership, Innovation, and Personal Resilience

Compelled to resign to quiet the election year uproar over the management of a training conference in Las Vegas, Martha Johnson, former Administrator of GSA, reveals the larger story of innovation underway in the agency. Her astute strategies for challenging bureaucratic myopia are explained alongside her highly personal story of resilience, two valuable lessons for leaders who want to make a big difference in the world.

Watch for Ms. Johnson's next book, *Interrupt: Startling an Organization into Change,* due for release in 2014.

Engage with Martha Johnson at
www.MarthaJohnson.com.

Leadership, Innovation,
& Personal Resilience

ON MY
WATCH

Martha Johnson

Former Administrator
U.S. General Services Administration

DUDLEY
COURT
PRESS

Published by:
Dudley Court Press, LLC
PO Box 102
Sonoita, AZ 85637
www.DudleyCourtPress.com

Cover Photo: Davidhartcorn.com"
Cover and Interior Design by M. Urgo

ISBN for perfectbound paperback format: 9781940013084
ISBN for electronic book (EPub format):   9781940013091
ISBN for limited edition hardcover: 9781940013015

LCCN: 2013949051

Publisher's Cataloging-in-Publication Data:

Johnson, Martha (Martha N.), 1952-
    On my watch : leadership, innovation, and personal resilience / Martha Johnson. –
Sonoita, AZ : Dudley Court Press, 2013.

    p. ; cm.

    ISBN: 978-1-940013-08-4 (paper) ;978-1-940013-01-5 (hardcover) ;
    978-1-940013-09-1 (ePub)

    Summary: Compelled to resign to quiet the election year uproar over the
    management of a training conference in Las Vegas, Martha Johnson, former
    Administrator of GSA (2010-2012), reveals the larger story of innovation underway
    in the agency. "On My Watch" illuminates her tenure in the Obama Administration
    and explains her leadership strategies of interruption, transparency, design, and
    blockbuster moves in the face of bureaucratic myopia, alongside her highly personal
    story of resilience, providing valuable lessons for leaders who want to make a big
    difference in the world–Publisher.

    1. Johnson, Martha (Martha N.), 1952- 2. United States. General Services
    Administration--Management. 3. United States. General Services Administration--
    Reorganization. 4. Leadership. 5. Organizational change. 6. Resilience (Personality
    trait) 7. Administrative agencies–United States–Management. 8. Administrative
    agencies--United States--Reorganization. 9. Public administration–United States.
    10. Bureaucracy–United States. 11. United States–Politics and government–2009-
    I. Title.

    JK1672 .J64 2013   2013949051
    352.5/30973--dc23   1310

To engage with Martha Johnson, please visit her website: www.MarthaJohnson.com

DEDICATION

To my beloved family—every opinionated, loyal, funny, curious, supportive, irritating, evolving, thoughtful, committed, stubborn, and caring one of you.

I love you to the moon and back.

There's lots of ways of playing.
There's a way of playing safe,
there's a way of using tricks and
there's the way I like to play
which is dangerously where
you're going to take a chance
on making mistakes in order to
create something you haven't
created before.

Dave Brubeck

CONTENTS

PREFACE

I love leading. And I loved leading the U.S. General Services Administration. I absolutely loved it.

I was the right match for it—the right person in the right place at the right time. I knew GSA from a previous five-year stint there during the Clinton Administration. Not many people are lucky enough to be appointed to lead government organizations in which they have spent significant time. I already knew the alphabet soup jargon and many of the players.

I also understood and believed in GSA's potential to make a big difference. This was no pipedream. GSA is a big box of support for government ranging from the courts and the executive branch all the way to states and tribal nations. I am not kidding about the big box thing. GSA's contracts and budgets add up to between $60 and $90 *billion* annually, larger than the annual GDP of fully two thirds of the countries in the world.

To top it off, President Obama's team clearly appreciated that GSA was a strategic asset to the Administration, not just a back office operation with a "Mops and Cops" nickname. Because the White House had large expectations of the agency, in business terms we were *aligned* in our goals and intentions. In other words, the potential of the agency and the leadership I could bring were matched with higher-up support.

During my work as part of the Obama Transition Team directly after the 2008 election, I researched the current problems at GSA. What I observed was as follows: a quarter of the executive positions were empty, strategy was nonexistent, major customers viewed their partnership with GSA askance, labor relations were acrimonious, the information technology infrastructure was inadequate, the schedules and other contract vehicles were burdensome, the Federal Acquisition Institute had atrophied, government-wide policy lacked focus, and the more expensive leasing portfolio was disproportionately large. Nearly two years had elapsed without a confirmed Administrator.

All in all, there were major possibilities and *huge* challenges waiting for me when I became the Administrator. It was the kind of opportunity that leaders dream of. I was in my element! I knew I would have the time of my life.

ACKNOWLEDGMENTS

Two people have been key to this book's particular messages of leadership and innovation. The first is Dave Barram, GSA's Administrator from 1996-2000. He is a fearless innovator and challenged GSA to play a more strategic role in helping government. His disarming curiosity pulled people into the game with him. He has been my boss, friend, and unwavering supporter, and I am forever indebted to him.

The second is Bob Peck, who served twice as GSA's Commissioner of the Public Buildings Service. Bob believes that well-designed public buildings support and enliven our democratic capabilities. His creativity and courage in service of that vision were infectious. He was a great Commissioner. I owe him my deepest appreciation.

While writing can mean days of solitude I have never been truly alone in this venture. Many people have had their hands on my shoulder. I have a passel of relatives, truckloads of friends, and rafts of colleagues to whom I owe individual and personal thanks. Forgive me for not naming each one of you.

This book emerged because of your support. If my ideas have any weight it is because you helped develop and sharpen them. If my sentences flow it is because you have nodded encouragement. If my heart comes through it is because you have opened yours to me.

Thank you.

Martha Johnson,
Annapolis, Maryland,
September 2013

INTRODUCTION

Sunday, February 7, 2010

Annapolis was buried under two feet of snow, and I could not travel the 35 miles to Washington. I was on hold again. For over a year I had been in line to assume a political appointment to lead the General Services Administration (GSA), reporting to President Barack Obama. After a ten-month delay, the United States Senate had finally voted unanimously to confirm me, and then the entire capital region had been shut down by heavy winter weather. I needed to get to D.C. to be sworn in.

"I've double-checked. We can do it over the phone," the lawyer said. "So get your husband inside, and he can hold the Bible." We had been shoveling snow outside all morning.

I shouted out the front door, "Can you come in for a minute? I can take the oath over the phone." Steve was talking with a neighbor. They waved to indicate that they had heard and both men started trudging to the door. Other neighbors turned at my call and waved as well. The snow had forced everyone outside to clear driveways and sidewalks. Many were taking the opportunity to gossip instead of shoveling.

Once inside, Bob pulled his cell phone out of his pocket. "Well, it's about time! How long have you been waiting on this job? How about if I take pictures?" We stood in the kitchen, dripping a bit with melting snow. As Steve held the phone I put my left hand on the Bible, raised the right one, and repeated the oath. Bob snapped a shot.

It was over in a minute. "Congratulations, Madam Administrator."

For a split second I wondered if the storm was an eerie predictor of what I was going to face in this new adventure. As my husband gave me a kiss, however, I let go of that worry. Instead, I knew that the practical, virtual, and unconventional swearing-in ceremony was a likely symbol of what I would be doing.

With that, we headed back outside to resume shoveling the mountains of snow.

Sunday, April Fools' Day, 2012

I was alone in the office, and it was deadly quiet. I was filling the boxes surrounding my chair with my personal belongings: an extra pair of shoes, a White House State Dinner menu, a fragment of a solar panel, business cards. I had a pile of mementos from my jam-packed two years as Administrator.

All of that activity was about to end very suddenly, however. I was packing up, because the next day I would resign from my position and my career as a public servant would be over. This was no April Fools' prank. This was one of those jokes that the Fates can play on a person.

It had been a fantastic run. GSA and I had been on a mission together. We were going to change the world by nudging the federal government into the future. In the middle of our trajectory of great progress, however, a rope had snapped in the organization's rigging, setting off a destructive snarl in the sails. As a result, I was walking the plank.

Two days earlier, I had met with the White House Chief of Staff, Jack Lew, for a final discussion about an emerging scandal. The GSA Inspector General (IG) was about to release a report regarding contracting errors and excessive spending on a GSA training conference held in Las Vegas in 2010. In addition to bent rules and immoderate costs, the poor judgment that peppered the event promised media mockery and easy glee from the political opposition.

The meeting with Lew started as an assessment of the situation. We ticked through the possible responses. As we talked, I noticed the budding leaves on the tree outside the window, but the options emerging to quiet the story in an election year were few. In the end, my resignation was the last card on the table. "Think about it over the weekend," he offered. But it was decided, and I knew it.

Stepping down would be a major and unexpected turn of events. My plan now was to spend the next day formally accepting the IG report, explicitly agreeing with its findings and the corrections needed, and signing letters announcing disciplinary actions against the senior people involved. After those meetings and signatures, I intended to call my senior staff together, explain the decisions, and say a brief goodbye.

Rehearsing the sequence, I mechanically took down the pictures and notices hanging on my cubicle wall. Monday would be a miserable day. I did not want to compound the torture with desk cleaning at the end of it.

As all leaders know, it is a complicated world. We try to make sense of it, yet bad/good things happen to good/bad people no matter how much we trace motivations and circumstances. Yes, GSA had begun to blossom, but something had happened in a corner of the organization in an election year. It was a collision of situations. As the Administrator, the politically appointed leader, I was ultimately accountable for what happened in the organization, including any political freight it spilled.

When I finished taping the boxes shut, my coffee mug still sat on the desk. Made of delicate bone china and painted with roses, it had been with me since my days as a factory manager in the 1980s. I picked it up, reflecting once again that its fragility was a bit of an illusion. How many adventures and job changes had it survived with me? Here we were at another juncture. I wrapped it carefully and stowed it in my purse.

What You'll Find in This Book

What happened in between those two scenes is the primary material for this book. GSA is situated at the very structural heart of the federal government, positioned and commissioned to help it work better. I had two years as its leader to gun for that goal. America longs for an effective, high-performing government, and I had a shot at improving the odds of hitting the target.

My story is not one of naive vision but of calculated creativity. Our big institutions—both public and private—need new approaches to stay vital. Therefore, the book's first section, Steering the Ship Forward, is about leveraging creativity in the face of the enormous constraints all organizational leaders face.

I begin by devoting chapters to three significant constraints and offering new angles for understanding and tackling them. The first two are ones I faced every day at GSA: the lack of full information and the distortion inherent in leading an extremely big organization.

The third is peculiar to leading government organizations. I devote a full chapter to this discussion in part to tip my hat to public sector leaders. Also, when *government* leaders can find game-changing solutions in organizations crammed full of constraints, *all leaders* should be encouraged and inspired to do more.

Leaving behind the litany of constraints, I turn, in Chapter Four, to shine a light on three specific examples of magnificent innovation we tapped at GSA. These *blockbuster ideas* have great relevance for business, government, and community organizations.

Anyone intent on changing up the game, however, is dealing in risk. In section two, Walking the Plank, and section three, Surfacing, I offer my personal thoughts about being a leader when things fall apart. By sharing how I came through the crisis myself, I hope to equip leaders with some personal strategies as they step into the fray.

On My Watch draws particularly on my stories about government leadership, yet it is relevant to leaders in any sector of society. I wrote it for current as well as aspiring leaders who must push boundaries. While my experience is only one story of leadership, it is laced with archetypal challenges as well as creative possibilities.

Our institutions must not only change, they must change dramatically and *perpetually*. If leaders are frozen in place by an obeisance to constraints or narrow self-protection, we will simply not succeed as an economy or as a nation. Our innovative competence is a national treasure. All leaders must champion it skillfully.

The GSA Back-Story

In order to provide you with some context, here's a quick review of the events that led to my resignation.

For a number of years, GSA's Public Buildings Service held a biannual training conference for a couple hundred members of the staff from the four western regions that covered Texas to the state of Washington.

The conference was purposefully cross-regional. The scale of GSA created a constant need for building relationships and improving communications among its parts to support better performance.

Internal collaboration was also a necessity for GSA because of its role in helping *all of government* innovate. The agency's customers were stationed across the country. Introducing them to change through more efficient and effective methods, technology, products, or workspace required GSA to speak with one voice, no matter where the client connection took place. This required strong bonds among GSA employees. Holding internal conferences to emphasize teamwork and information sharing was a steppingstone to an innovative government.

The 2010 training event was held in Las Vegas, Nevada, an economical option given the travel and hotel rates offered to the government. Planning and contracting for the conference began in 2009, well before I was in office. The executives that designed and/or sponsored it were two levels below me on the organizational chart. I did not attend the conference.

There were run-of-the-mill conditions that put me in the dark about the event. It would have been somewhat unusual for me to be in the loop. Not impossible, but unusual. With 13,000 employees, thousands of contractors, a dozen discrete business lines, White House initiatives, and a host of innovative programs and operational challenges under my purview, a training event was only a pixel on my screen in my first six months in office.

Soon after the conference took place in October 2010, GSA's Deputy Administrator, my second-in-command, asked the GSA Inspector General to take a look at it. Inspectors General (IG) are internal government auditors who report both to the President and the U.S. Congress. They check whether an organization has complied with government policy and avoided misconduct, waste, fraud, or abuse. They are available if the agency leadership wants a third party view on a matter.

The Deputy Administrator had questions about casual stories she had heard of a bicycle exercise at the Las Vegas training conference. She was well within the bounds of her executive position to make the request of the IG.

In February 2012, over 15 months later, he gave me a draft of his report so that I could formally review it and include a response when he issued it publicly.

He reported that, yes, teams of people had assembled bicycles at the Las Vegas training conference. The exercise had been a way to illuminate lessons for collaboratively working together on a task. In the course of asking about that, he learned that the bikes were subsequently donated to charity, but government rules had been stretched in the process. A consultant had purchased and then donated the bikes. If the government had handled the bikes, it would have been obliged to follow more formal procedures about the disposal of government property.

The IG had dug further and went on to name additional contracting violations that were uncovered. One, for example, squared an early deal between the government and the Las Vegas hotel where the conference was held—in favor of the hotel. This adjustment was done, apparently, when the government per diem reimbursement rates had been adjusted downward. Federal employees are given a travel cost schedule (ironically, GSA sets, manages, and adjusts that schedule) that dictates how much they can claim for reimbursement against their meals and lodging.

In what appeared to be a wink, the hotel reduced its room rate from the earlier agreement, while the government agreed to make up the difference in other areas, such as the overall food contract. The outcome of that arrangement included some fancy appetizers at a reception. Hence, expensive sushi was part of the scandal.

Of additional concern was the report's revelation that some of the ideas and decisions regarding the conference had come from a relative of one of the public officials in charge. Government money is always and only to be spent by government people.

The report also detailed excessive travel costs associated with the conference. A chunk was for multiple trips taken by planners to see the Las Vegas hotel and develop the conference agenda and content.

Some of the report was less about extravagance and violations of law than about poor judgment rooted in the planners' insulated attitude and a deaf ear to public perception. For example, the hotel "comped" fancy suites for some of the attending executives. This means that some expensive rooms were assigned to the conference, and the rates were reduced as part of a common industry practice when any group rents a large block of rooms. Such issues raised eyebrows more than they violated the law.

The report was picked up by the media and struck the raw nerve of politics. Headlines proliferated about irresponsible and extravagant federal employees. The spoofs and skits in the conference's awards ceremony went viral. Soon committees on the Hill were jostling over who would hold the first Congressional hearing.

It was all there: innovation, politics, performance, information sharing, colossal organizations, and the role of leaders.

PART ONE

STEERING THE SHIP FORWARD

For the past 25 years I have lived in Annapolis, Maryland, home of the U.S. Naval Academy. While it is a city of recreational sailors who enjoy the harbor and the extraordinary beauty of the Chesapeake Bay, it is also a city filled most of the year with young men and women in summer working whites or full dress blues. They are preparing for leadership responsibilities at sea.

I often watch them run by our house on their exhausting workouts, and I think about the strenuous training they are experiencing in and out of the classroom. No matter how much is condensed into their four years at the Academy, they will be innovating and adjusting from those initial lessons throughout their careers.

Their success will depend on their flexibility and creativity in all sorts of settings. Like all our future leaders, they will often be leading in the dark without good information. Many of them will find themselves in large organizations that will scramble their usual perspectives and sense of proportion. Whatever their positions, they will inevitably interact with government and its highly determined environment. Each challenge can sharpen their skills.

As they learn to wring opportunity out of challenges, they will also thrive if they can pour forth a fresh stream of creative ideas that incessantly pushes possibilities into being. Both coping *and* creating are the hallmarks of great leaders.

In the continuum of my own development as a leader, I bumped into many lessons of navigating cleverly through difficult shoals as well as hoisting sails to find new lands. While I was at GSA I grew to understand even more. In this section, I offer what I consider now to be some of the most valuable lessons of my leadership voyage.

CHAPTER ONE
Leading in the Dark

As a leader I was often in the dark, and I was not an unusual leader. The unvarnished reality is that most leaders work in the dark.

Like most leaders, I do not like to be in the dark, and I worked hard to be informed. I wanted to know, learn, and be smart about the organization I led. My wonderful and dedicated team at GSA took seriously their task of briefing me on anticipated issues or breaking news. Notes and updates came to me 24/7. I stayed up at night digesting hefty memos. I spent hundreds of hours meeting with customers, industry leaders, lawmakers, and employees to hear their issues and points of view. My blog was loaded with readers' comments.

The twist is that the speed and volume of information create the illusion that information is readily available. Leaders scramble honestly to get out of the shadows, yet many factors conspire to block or adjust information. Briefings can be shortchanged by time constraints or poor preparation. The flow of data can be sporadic or dated. Some delays are happenstance. Few of the information hiccups, in my experience, are genuinely malicious. All of them, however, are frustrating.

There is risk for leaders in not understanding this reality. It is supremely naive or shows inexperience not to grasp that information is pruned, adjusted, colored, slowed, or just plain withheld. Leaders inevitably work under some cloak of darkness.

Quantity is not the only problem or even the main problem. Leaders cannot assimilate all the necessary information into an orderly or proper map. Brilliant analysts plug away at the job but are always staggering into the wind. There is some hope for the new capabilities associated with Big Data, which captures and displays the sandstorm of information. We are learning more and more about separating the signal from the noise. The quest for *understanding*, however, will continue to be difficult and illusive.

Leaders these days must adhere to a hard-and-fast rule. Information management should be near, if not at the top of, the agenda. Leaders probably will never fully solve how to deal with massive amounts of information, nor can they give up on the effort, but they can be smarter about it.

This chapter explores some of this darker side of the information age. Information seems to be everywhere but somehow not always in front of leaders. Leaders have choices, however, and among those are strategies to encourage more transparency in organizations and to employ measures that reveal progress and direction rather than simply tabulate activity.

Why Information Flow ... Isn't

Back in the 1980s, I was a young pup manager in a Cummins Engine Company factory. We were doing great things: our diesel engine assembly process was innovative; we were reinventing our systems to reduce mistakes and excessive costs; and by disciplining the supply chain and training employees, we were systematically producing a higher quality product. As a bonus, the plant's leaders were competent and responsible. I was soaking up wonderful career-shaping lessons.

The factory was nestled in a slight valley below a well-trafficked county road. Its roof was as large as six football fields and in plain sight from the road. One day I was out on the factory floor walking along the assembly line with a couple of other managers. We were on our way to the Plant Operating Team meeting, affectionately known as the POT. Glancing at the workers on the line, one manager shook his head and told us that he had learned that two of his employees were spending their lunch breaks on the factory roof having sex. He was both laughing at and bemoaning the situation.

We grinned sympathetically. "Better fix that one fast. Gawd, if Kevin ever finds out, he'll have a heart attack!"

That was an understatement. Kevin was the plant manager and our boss' boss. No, Kevin should never find out. And the sex-on-the-roof-thing had to stop—at all levels.

In other words, while the manager had to read the riot act to the trysting couple *immediately*, the rest of us had to keep our mouths clamped shut. That was the code in the organization. We knew what Kevin expected. He was not an uptight guy, just a good family man and a solid plant manager. He set norms, we agreed with them, and we were responsible for seeing them represented in our behavior and performance. We did not want to disappoint him or get him angry.

Managers in organizations everywhere live with versions of a Do-Not-Tell-the-Leader Code. In this case there were typical dynamics at play. Everyone had a lot to do, and Kevin did not expect to hear about the detail of every decision or operation. It was not efficient, for starters.

We were also starkly realistic. We did not intend to tell Kevin, because we did not need to *increase* the problem. It was obvious that this was an over-the-top situation. Kevin was bound to be upset, offended, and potentially embarrassed within the larger community. When a nerve is touched, there is usually a reflexive action in response. We knew that he would insist on a unilateral fix. Someone could get fired or policies could get tightened. We could lose some managerial autonomy. Therefore, and without much ado, we managers agreed to fix the situation and stay mum about it. Zip the lips. Code Silent.

Was I right in sticking with Code Silent? Had I been a more mature manager, would I have come up with a better solution? If I had been in Kevin's job, what would I have wanted the managers to do?

There is no perfect answer, and each situation requires judgment. The lesson for me was huge, however. Organizations simply do not tell their leaders everything. Leaders must wise up if they aren't already smart about this. Employees regularly make decisions about what should be sent up the ladder and what should stop with them.

Without Perfect Information

In college I had a macroeconomics professor who was extraordinarily animated and theatrical. He would lecture us with a wagging finger that we would never, never, *never* have enough information for truly proper decision making. Delaying decisions in a quest for perfect information was a fool's errand. "You must find a way to work in the haze."

Without perfect information, leaders have to make guesses and take risks. It is not at all easy. I must confess that as GSA's Administrator I lost very little sleep over actually taking a risk. That was in part because I rarely took a risk by myself. Many of the tough decisions I had to make were well vetted and laid out for me. I walked into them with my eyes wide open, having received and digested significant analysis. The odds were usually pretty good, or at least I was very clear about them.

However, I was uneasy about the risks that I *did not know* I was taking. They were a different deal altogether. My ego could handle making the wrong decisions when I had been briefed and had sifted the options. The difficulty lay in my low-level-rumbling concern about *not knowing something that needed correction.* What about the risks that were hidden from me—out of sight for whatever benign or not so benign reason? It was a worrisome thought and always there. What crocodile was lurking just below the waterline?

Being in the dark makes a leader edgy: bad edgy, not good edgy. Leaders will rarely admit to this, of course, but it is the truth, whether revealed or not. One very seasoned executive who ran a $20 billion enterprise said quietly to me when we were commiserating about this problem at a dinner party, "Don't kid yourself, Martha. Every day I go to work and I wonder, *Is this the day*? Is some egregious mistake or individual wrongdoing going to surface that is a surprise to me but I will have to resign?"

The edginess can turn into an urge to control. The challenge of controlling an organization is dicey business, however. Organizations are human, not mechanical. Asserting controls, whether physical, mental, behavioral, or financial, is a complicated undertaking. If done poorly, the effort can backfire. Power asserted can easily become power resented, power contested, and power denied.

When a leader becomes intent on control, it is possible for the organization to seize up. I have seen a memo from a Chief Operating Officer insisting on cost controls on all supplies including paper clips. Not surprisingly, nothing significant came of it, and I suspect that his concerns were not quelled.

Do not get me wrong. Organizations must have systemic controls and guards. No organization can live without proper boundaries, contracts, and agreements. But leaders need better alternatives than indulging their anxiety about their lack of information by asserting controls and hounding employees.

Those behaviors can set off a doom loop. When leaders try to assert micro-control, demanding exhausting detail, they send the message that they do not trust employees. In return, the organization will not trust the leader and will react accordingly. As leaders bear down, organizations respond by not responding. Employees make themselves invisible or become parsimonious with what they know. Leaders find themselves further bereft of information. Their darkness deepens and the cycle continues.

How Information Can Get Choked in Government

Factories are hardly the only arenas in which staff blocks information from flowing to leaders. In government it is not uncommon for the career employees to stall information on its way to their political superiors. Often the reason for this is the "B Team" strategy summarized in the slogan, "I will *be* here when you are gone." In other words, it takes too much effort to brief, train, and acclimate the political leadership. Too often the appointed leaders are on a merry-go-round anyway and disappear after only a short stay.

One government manager described this to me with great hilarity over a beer. "We work hard to convince the political guys that they are at the center of things. We give them decision memos to sign and thick briefing books to read. We set them up with young employees to be an audience for their stories.

"They think they are driving the organization like a car, pressing the pedals and using the signal lights. If you look under the hood, however (hee hee, ha ha), you will see the careerists madly cranking the engine and operating the car. Little is actually hooked up for the driver to operate."

In addition legal and regulatory constraints keep government leaders in the dark. For example, as Administrator I was excluded from most of the selection process for hiring a new executive. Government rules are structured to prevent unnecessarily heavy political influence in employment decisions.

Contracting rules can be similarly excluding. For instance, as Administrator, I was appropriately cut out of the negotiations over choosing a development company to renovate and upgrade the historic Old Post Office Pavilion on Pennsylvania Avenue. Only when the GSA contracting team was ready to announce publicly the company designated to prepare a more complete proposal and plan did I learn that it would be the Trump Organization.

The size of government also presents problems. With international operations, 11 domestic regions, dozens of field offices, and thousands of buildings, GSA was so spread out that I could hardly hope to visit all of its corners, much less know all that was going on.

To help with this problem, GSA had a structure for a trusted pipeline of information flow into headquarters. Each GSA region was allocated a political appointee to be my eyes and ears. Ironically, the White House did not name a person until 2011 to lead the Pacific Rim Region, the region responsible in 2009–2010 for the Las Vegas training conference.

Any number of factors can put a chokehold on information. It is no wonder that leaders are often in the dark. It probably is a wonder that they get much information at all.

Interrupt: A Leadership Strategy for Change

Organizations caught in this tight spin of difficulties need new possibilities. Doom loops are like old record players that would hit a scratch on a vinyl record and play the same bit of music over and over and over. Someone had to nudge the needle to the next groove to stop the repetition. When things get stuck in organizations, looping and looping, leaders need ways to move the needle, by inserting fresh thinking and new options.

I call this *interrupting*. It is a powerful strategy for leaders whose organizations are stuck and need to tackle entrenched problems. I want to offer a brief look at the strategy and offer a way in which interrupting can help with the problem of leading in the dark.

Interrupting is a softball way to find new openings, giving a smidgen of new energy and possibility to a stymied situation. While leaders are often expected to grab the reins, pull hard, and turn the entire stagecoach around, such strategies can be overly dramatic, take too much effort or time, and throw up a lot of mud and wreckage in the process.

Instead, leaders can employ interruptions. Importantly, *interruptions are not disruptions*. They are simple, often very small actions that can change the way we talk about, see, approach, or formulate a problem, which can then lead to further simple, easy-to-adopt changes. It is about getting started, about planting seeds.

Putting something, however small, into motion is the seminal act, and often the hardest thing to do in the face of tough challenges. Importantly, interruptions signal a capacity for risk taking, a curiosity about what might happen, and an appetite for moving forward. All of this together adds up to a formula for real change.

The beauty of interruptions is that leaders are in a position to view organizations as entire systems. Anyone with such a *systems perspective* appreciates that there are many overlapping reinforcing ties that keep the status quo as it is. Introducing a handful of interruptions is like pinging a system on multiple sides, and that can lead first to a mild and then a more vigorous shake-up. While interruptions can be small or simple, they can start a process that leads to substantial change, even transformation.

It is difficult to catalog all of the possible sorts of interruptions. Therein, frankly, lies their genius. Leaders can interrupt just about anything: they can change words, setting, arrangements, sequencing, or a host of other elements. It is a valuable practice to be regularly on the lookout for points of interruption. Dare I suggest that it can introduce fun into otherwise dour situations?

Leaders Interrupting Themselves

One of the skills leaders need to bring to the table is the ability to *interrupt themselves.*

The power and position of a leader can stand in the way of an organization's grasping a new direction if the leader is not flexible and open personally. Leaders' behaviors tend to be magnified across the organization. This can be trouble when leadership behaviors are bad ones. For example, when a leader yells at staff, everyone soon knows about it. If the yelling continues, the organization's norms will shift, as people interpret the leader's signal that yelling is appropriate. Others will soon be yelling as well.

Similarly, if leaders exhibit fear or nervousness about their lack of information, the organization will sense it and react. Information will start to get bollixed up. Feeling the intensity from above, some employees might hide or hold their cards in a protective move while others might flood the leader with information. Importantly, information flow will be about appeasing the leader, not about informing the organization. It will inevitably be distorted because it is motivated improperly.

Unfortunately, if leaders behave badly, few staff members are positioned in the hierarchy to intervene or confront them about it. When those behaviors perpetuate the darkness, so to speak, leaders will neither be informed, nor will they necessarily recognize their own role in the cycle.

Interrupting oneself is, therefore, important in changing this dynamic. Such interruptions can be structured in many ways with coaches, third party feedback, or personal boards of directors. Self-awareness, however pursued, is crucial for leaders who are intent on interrupting organizations.

Interrupting with Descriptions

Most of the interruptions I explore in this book start with finding new ways to *describe* a problem. I deeply believe that changing the characterization of a problem will change the thinking about it. If a problem is re-described or restated, people may begin to see something in a new way and find new ways to respond to it. Soon the interruptions will spawn more interruptions.

Interruptions can range well beyond words. I also use physical arrangements, visuals, music, meeting design, tokens, and anything else that occurs to me. The basic rule of thumb is to keep it simple, give it a try, see what sticks, and keep on going.

Returning to my favorite interruption, how does a leader find new ways to describe a problem? Many techniques exist to do this. Importantly, leaders do not have to *originate* new language or personally reframe the problem, but they do have to see that such a reconfiguration is done.

One way is for leaders to ask for internal brainstorming processes to break out new ways of seeing a problem. Another way is to hire consultants to bring a different and external view, for they are better positioned to see angles that the internal people cannot.

Leaders can also request that a problem be mapped so that it can literally be viewed from different and unusual perspectives. Placing the problem visually at the center of a network of people and processes can help dislodge chronic misinterpretations or closed thinking. Multiple interruption points can be identified.

Here are two examples that suggest how powerful it can be simply to jostle the typical associations held with a problem:

- We call it dirty fishpond water. Could it also be nutrition for a hydroponic garden?

- We call it a crying baby. Could it also be an exercising baby?

Reconceptualization can do wonders. Worlds of creative possibilities are suddenly available.

Interrupting with Questions

Another possible approach is to recast problems by employing a few basic questions.

Good leaders understand—or at least insist on exploring—the bigger picture: the vision (what), the full community that is touched (who), the broader time frame (when), the needs, desires, and hopes involved (why), and the challenge presented (how). Any of those questions can help interrupt a situation that is stuck.

Here is how it might work with the problem of leading in the dark.

Try the first question. What is the vision? Instead of defining the problem as an obstacle (darkness) that signals the preeminence of the constraints, leaders should be calling the play and naming the vision.

They can express the situation as a call for something better. They can switch channels from an obstacle to a goal. The problem does not need to be about being stuck in the dark, but instead, about finding a way to get into the *light*. A goal of aiming for the light puts the excitement of a dream into the mix. The simple interruption of changing out the word "dark" for the word "light" opens many possibilities.

Let's move to the next question of *who* is involved. Does the problem belong solely to the leader? Leaders are not the only ones who struggle with misinformation and hidden information. People in organizations chronically complain that no one tells them anything, yet information is regularly demanded of them. They have to take surveys, fill out tedious forms, and chronicle their time, whereabouts, mileage, and expenses. They cringe as information goes up the line without sufficient explanation. The mismatch of information and understanding can be profound, with employees often suffering the consequences.

Instead of chasing shadows, exhibiting paranoia, and focusing on what they themselves do not know, leaders can open up a broader view of *who* may be touched, suffering, or rendered less effective by the darkness. Shifting questions in this way invites partners who may be similarly frustrated and hoping for a different outcome. They will have reason to join in the effort and find some solidarity as well as contribute additional ideas, abilities, and energy. Again, with the simple interruption of asking the question (*who*), which yields "we" instead of "me," the likelihood of progress increases.

A couple of interrupting questions can produce new answers and change the entire landscape. When the leader points forward (*Shall we head for the light and not wallow in the dark?*) and is inclusive (*This problem is painful for everyone*), the organization can sense creative leadership at work. Leaders become leaders, and the organization has much more reason to join in the work ahead. The challenge becomes *leading the organization into the light.*

Reframed in this manner, the problem of leading the organization into the light invites at least two ideas for proceeding: a strategy of transparency and a more purposeful use of measures. Let's look at each of these strategies and how they played out at GSA.

Leading the Organization *toward the Light*: Transparency

During the rise of industrial America, company foremen would place people in jobs next to people who spoke different languages. This mixing was purposeful, intended to block the diverse immigrant workforce from communicating with each other and possibly organizing themselves into unions.

While among the most blatant, this example illustrates how historically our organizations have discouraged lateral communication and coordination. As a result, business and government organizations have been substantially if not strictly hierarchical. The military model of command and control has historically pervaded much of our organized enterprise. Authority, responsibility, power, and information flowed vertically.

Over the years and for all sorts of reasons, organizations have been evolving into flatter and more collaborative structures. Technology has been the chief spark plug, freeing up information and opening windows into organizations from multiple angles. Social change, broader education, new ownership structures, and a host of other things have been important influencers as well. Consequently, our organizations are ripe for heightened transparency, both internally and externally.

Early in its tenure the Obama Administration placed expectations on the government to open up and share more information, thereby increasing its transparency. At GSA we, like the rest of the government, were expected to open up more of our communications and information for others to access and explore.

In addition, GSA was handed responsibility to help build technical and policy capacity across the government for a more transparent federal government. No longer should leaders and organizations play a cat-and-mouse game for information. Information was not to be a hoarded treasure, but a channel for better work results. In other words, the president was explicitly asking that we *lead our government organizations into the light*. A significant interruption was at hand.

Transparency as a Culture and Strategy for GSA

What does it take to advance transparency in an organization? In the case of government, there was already some scar tissue about transparency. The Freedom of Information Act (FOIA) of 1966 ordered more openness in government. It has been hard, however, to legislate or direct transparency successfully. Lots of forces continue to bear down and narrow information flow. The FOIA has itself been modified with numerous exemptions. The government bureaucracy has struggled with organizational resistance (people dislike being watched) and the sheer cost of openness (finding, cataloging, posting, and maintaining records).

At GSA there were many levers other than legislation that could be pulled to build transparency into the system. Both the organization's culture and business strategy could be deepened and strengthened with an emphasis on openness and sharing.

This would be an adjustment, however. For much of its 60-year existence, GSA had stayed mostly below the radar and out of sight. It did not receive much press and was not a household acronym. I often got laughs during speeches when I explained that I was from GSA, which was neither the Girl Scouts of America nor the Gay-Straight Alliance.

GSA's less-than-celebrity profile was largely due to its role as a support organization for the rest of government. Its job was to help public agencies to deliver on *their* program missions. While GSA's culture has always included elements of an innovative spirit and a strong sense of community pride, it also sported a healthy measure of self-protection. It has scars from being treated like the downstairs staff. Or, as our Public Buildings Commissioner would say, "No one loves the landlord."

Transparency could help. Placing a stronger value on openness, the agency could encourage employees to tell their stories and describe accomplishments. The results could be not just a boost in employee pride but also a way to enhance engagement with customers. Frankly, sharing more and inviting outsiders to see in would also put the agency more on its toes.

A business strategy of transparency led in additional and productive directions. GSA took the specific step of moving early to the cloud, which led to much easier information sharing among employees and with customers. Employees had more consistent access to programs and databases and were able to be more flexible and mobile as they worked and supported customers.

The technology also supported a dramatic increase in collaboration. Employees were able to form hundreds of online communities, virtually solve problems with large participant groups, and use shared document features. In addition to working more productively and collectively, GSA was able to show the government that such technology and work did not compromise security.

The cloud technology, the improved information flow, and the increasing collaboration skills proved a great help to the GSA communications and public relations staff in researching, cataloging, and sharing stories, updates, and information internally and externally. Thus transparency built on itself.

In addition to building a framework and capability for transparency, leaders can do a lot with their behaviors and other creative nudges and jostles to the system.

Leading Transparency: Modeling and Language

Preaching about transparency is a one-way activity. Exhorting people gets old fast, so the organization tunes out. Leaders do well to *act* in line with the values they want to embed. Setting explicit expectations is one thing, but modeling those expectations sends a message more likely to be heard and imitated.

Visiting a Kawasaki plant in Nebraska in the 1980s, I bumped into my first dramatic example of a leader modeling transparency and visibility. The plant manager regularly jumped on the back of the floor-washing machine circling the assembly line so he could see things up close without distracting workers.

Years later, at Touchstone Consulting Group the firm's partners engaged in a "hot wash" to yield lessons learned from a client visit. Their aggressive honesty about what they felt they could have done better themselves encouraged the rest of the staff to voice and learn from mistakes.

At GSA, I worked at being visible and accessible to convey that transparency was part of my job. I blogged regularly about all sorts of subjects, including my own commuting habits, reading lists, and budget news. A blog is hardly a revolutionary idea now, but at that time it was not yet very common in government.

It was also a great way to engage everyone in new ideas. As I regularly shared my thoughts with the organization, people became more inclined to respond. I exchanged emails with all sorts of employees and made a point to participate actively in ideation events. I was also quick to respond on chat lines and good conversations took place. When leaders open up, the organization can, too.

I made another very simple gesture for transparency by giving my speeches from outlines instead of reading from scripts. Talking invites response, whereas reading does not invite much give and take. People sensed the difference, and the Q&A sessions were always livelier.

Opaque language can stifle transparency. As I communicated with GSA I aimed for memorable alliteration and clever slogans in order to make ideas fresh and more likely to be noticed. For example, I promoted a new way to behave by using the phrase "Yell Up and Not Down." It was another form of the Don't-Shoot-the-Messenger maxim. The phrase was a direct appeal for more transparency. I wanted to interrupt the embedded norm that good news flows up, while bad news flows down.

I had no illusions that a phrase by itself would make GSA transparent. However, it could post notice. It could catch on and spread. In this particular case, I noticed that people started to frame presentations and briefings with the introduction, "In the spirit of Yell Up and Not Down, I want to let you know ...." I was getting a little out of the shadows.

I was unrelenting with my "Martha-isms." Another phrase I used was "Fail Fast, Fail Forward, Fail Fruitfully." This pokes at the usual government practices of planning extensively, examining risks exhaustively, and being very careful to avoid failure. Transparency is impossible when fear of failure guarantees that success is the only topic of conversation.

That phrase helped me test whether failure and risk were something we could talk about. If the phrase spread into common speech, it would tell me that the idea had passed some test of acceptability. As it happened, "Fail Fast, Fail Forward, Fail Fruitfully" was quoted a lot, used in commentators' blogs, and even showed up in publications like the *Washington Post*. That was satisfying.

As a leader encouraging transparency, I needed the organization talking and sharing ideas and concepts easily. I preferred that people hear and practice new ideas on the run. Months after I left GSA, I received a note from a man who had worked at GSA for many years.

> Getting leaders and managers to unfreeze, to open themselves to change is no small task, yet you created an environment in which new ways of thinking, working, and behaving were possible and even welcomed. I smile when I find myself saying things like, "have the meeting in the meeting" or "work is what we do, not where we do it."

When new norms showed up in our daily chatter, well, hallelujah! The closed culture was being interrupted, new ideas were becoming commonplace, and if everyone was sharing them, transparency was happening.

Leading Transparency: Look In with Your Ears

The Herbert Clark Hoover Department of Commerce Building in Washington, D.C., was constructed between 1929 and 1932.

At the time it was the largest and most complex federal building in existence and probably the largest office building in the world. One of its features is an elevator near one of the building's western facing entrances that is labeled and presumably exclusively reserved for the use of the Secretary.

The goal was not protection and security. Rather, a Cabinet member was someone who in those days led the organization but didn't necessarily mix casually with its employees.

How unfortunate. Leaders actually *need* to be in human touch with organizations. Why trust leaders or tell them anything if they are invisible? It's not a game of chicken. The leader has to go first, opening up, sharing, walking around, being seen, blogging, hosting webinars, attending retirement parties, and so on. Leaders hold a big responsibility for *starting* the conversation.

However, it's more than that. If leaders want to know what is happening in organizations, they must create deliberate, open air space to *listen* to and *hear* from people. They might invite comments on blogs, welcome emails, or hold speed halls (not town halls) where any employee can line up to speak to them for three minutes. Communications will not change unless the leader models and acts in a new way. It is very simple: to get people to talk, leaders must shut up and listen.

And it works. In my first days at GSA I made a point of greeting employees at the door. It was a way to say hello and introduce myself. As hundreds of people poured through the turnstiles, I was delighted to recognize many faces.

An older gentleman introduced himself with a serious expression. "I think we are using dated cost structures with my product line." That was it—no name or hello. I looked him in the eye and said that if he wanted to tell me more, I would be happy to learn about it. A few days later a note from him arrived explaining the problem, and we were able to ask some questions and make some good changes.

Having a moment with a leader who is listening gives employees an opening to share. The small interruption promptly chases away some shadows and encourages transparency. Why wouldn't a leader want to make that possible?

Leading Transparency: Grab What Is Available

There is no particular reason to sit tight and wait for an orchestrated transparency program to unfold. I believe leaders should quit making everything so elaborate and over-planned. In business and in government, I saw too many leaders go for the big and complicated. New information technology policies, overhauled reporting structures, or high tech big data take a great deal of time, money, and more. Leaders try to be too clever by half; in so doing, they overwhelm possible new sprouts of change.

Once when I was a consultant, the firm handed me responsibility for a very demanding client in the national security field. I inherited a solid, though vastly understaffed, consulting team. The project had been plagued with staff turnover, and we were far short of the full complement of consultants required for the work. People were stressed and deadlines were looming. It was one of those times when employees cry in meetings.

Clearly, staffing was a root cause of many of the operational issues and I had to move quickly. Yet it takes a long time to hire and shift people. Talent is not like machinery that requires simply unbolting something here and re-bolting something there.

Because there was a lot on the line, I took the unconventional step of setting up something that I called a Day Trader Meeting, scheduled for 15 minutes every other day at noon. Anyone with a job to fill, a recommendation of someone to recruit, or interest in changing jobs could join the meeting. I posted the spreadsheet of open and filled positions, and together the group would work the problems.

Our little personnel stock exchange was unusual in its transparency. For some it was unsettling. How could I be so open about staffing decisions? To lessen concerns, I invited Human Resources to send a representative to the meeting to help manage discussions that verged into privacy or confidentiality matters.

The process caught on. Employees realized they had more opportunity and choice and something was happening to relieve the squeeze on staff. Managers could press their case about their staffing needs. More people began to show up for the Day Trader Meetings.

With all the relevant people participating, I could make decisions on the spot and communicate them immediately. The staffing pressures began to ease. The level of honest conversation in the organization also ticked up. Soon our staffing dilemmas completely receded, and the previously exotic idea of being open about staffing decisions became the norm. Transparency became routine.

Across organizations there are hundreds of routines, processes, and daily activities that can become more transparent without a huge amount of effort of orchestrated program. For example, I have worked in eight organizations, and every single one of them ran an annual, but largely hidden, exercise called performance planning. We all know the drill. Employees file lengthy, detailed plans. Presumably the content explains how a person's work and goals link to larger organizational goals. Once developed, the plans are a) reviewed and approved by the employees' managers and b) promptly filed away in a drawer. Incredibly, no one else ever sees them.

What about taking something pedestrian like performance planning and opening it up?

I asked GSA executives to pair up and tell each other about their performance plans. How hard an interruption was that? The response was unanimously positive. People got to know each other better, size up another's plan, and find new overlap and ways of sharing support. I think a little bit of competitive pride even stole into the conversations. The results of a minor gesture toward transparency built better relationships, improved the plans, and opened up the organization.

A simple glance around any organization will yield plenty of other opportunities for transparency: meeting protocols, schedules, office layout, customer interactions, packaging, titles, and departmental charters. Look around, make your own list, and get on with it.

Leading Transparency: Welcome Information in Other Forms

When I assumed responsibility for the understaffed consulting team, I had more to worry about than stressed employees. I also had to learn and absorb as much as possible about my new client organization—fast. In order to be credible at our first client meeting within days of starting the job, I had to ramp up. I also needed to understand the client in order to steer the consulting staff knowledgably.

Consultants are faced regularly with this boning-up challenge. The usual process involves getting formal briefings, interviewing key people, and reading the client's strategic plans. I was always on the hunt for more materials. Over time I found out about other sources of insight, other channels on the cable. Leaders should quiz consultants on how they get to know their client organizations, for there are tips to be learned about how to *see in fast*.

For example, every organization has its own jargon. It is possible to see into an organization by listening carefully to its words. In one of my client organizations employees tossed off the word "slavery" in everyday discourse. "Slavery" is an extremely strong and unusual word for day-to-day business. My team was curious about what people really meant.

The answer turned out to be illuminating. When we asked for clarification about it, we were told that it was meant to be taken as a joke. Wow! The cultural implication of an organization that joked about itself as slaves suggested a self-image of subservience, not of pride. This coincided with and confirmed our assessment of the client's attitude about its work quality.

If it isn't language, it can be pictures. A friend of mine who worked in industry before joining a college as a professor told me the following story. In the facility where she had worked, the managers regularly monitored the men's bathroom. Apparently one employee acted also as an underground artist who drew and posted cartoons about the people and events in the organization. The drawings were unvarnished depictions of incidents, issues, and people. It provided great information for the managers that obviously someone wanted them to have.

An organization's workspace—whether it is open, closed, shabby, or bright—can reveal a lot. At Touchstone Consulting Group I put a piano in our small lobby to signal our creativity to visitors and clients. When I visited the Costco headquarters years ago, we were seated around a very plain but serviceable table for our meeting with senior executives and served coffee in disposable cups. Their no-fuss, nothing-lavish approach told the Costco story even more than the briefing and numbers did. Seeing a huge picture of the earth as photographed from space hanging outside Ben and Jerry's main factory entrance, a visitor cannot miss the company's broad social commitment.

Seeing more deeply into organizations takes strategies, policies, skills, and insight. It also takes simply paying close attention. Transparency is a worthy goal that is not beyond reach. For leaders who recognize and fret about the limits of their information and knowledge, there are many creative ways to uncover what is hidden.

Leading the Organization *toward the Light*: Measures

Measures are a national obsession. We have embraced them as the Holy Grail, a silver bullet, and a winning lottery ticket. We hope they will tell us what is going on in our large and complicated world. Students are subjected to exhaustive testing so that we can understand what is happening in our schools. Politicians do not make a move without polling constituents. Measures are the ultimate swimming goggles, a way to look below the surface.

It does not take lots of leadership savvy to understand that measures are a great way to see into organizations, interpret what is happening, and ward off the problem of being in the dark. Measures are powerful tools, which give dimension and shape to activity in the organization. It is possible to measure revenue, quality, reliability, performance, output, and everything else under the sun. Legitimately hungry to know all they can, leaders use measures to gather point-specific information, spot trouble, see weakness, and monitor performance.

If measures seem like a goldmine, however, a leader needs to be very careful not to turn them into fool's gold. Yes, they offer the potential for understanding and light, but without an inclusive and disciplined approach to measures, they can actually *create more darkness.*

We all know the movie *E.T. the Extra-Terrestrial.* In the opening scenes, we see flashlights darting around the woods as people search the environs in the wake of a space ship landing. The lights, however, are terrifying to E.T., who is hiding huddled in the underbrush.

Measures can be like flashlights searching for information and knowledge. If poorly deployed, they turn into probes or interrogation lights that grill, shame, and terrorize people. They can send the organization back into the darkness of mistrust and fear.

Hunger for Measures Goes Overboard

Yes, unfortunately measures can get out of hand. In the name of better transparency, they can become a religion of their own, exhausting an organization, distorting purpose and activity, and, most importantly, creating a risk equation that kills innovation. People become so uneasy about being measured and watched that they freeze up and do not push boundaries or try new approaches.

The slippery slide to excess starts with oversight. Schools test pupils so that parents, administrators, the government, and the media can all watch and calibrate progress. There are signs that the testing is so extensive that it is exhausting students and undermining teachers. The exacting tests have led to hints of cheating, as well as compromises to dumb down tests or waive reports.

A raft of interest groups demands all sorts of measurements from both public and private organizations. Leaders and managers are expected to issue reports about revenue, cost trends, safety performance, trade patterns, and a thousand other items to shareholders, citizens, regulators, oversight bodies, auditors, interest groups, and consumer advocates. Big Brother seems to be the new norm.

Caught in the searchlights, organizations scramble. Employees accommodate, anticipate, and even try to head off the probes. Leaders play defense. They release favorable measurement trends and play the game of statistics vigorously. As one government executive told me, "I collect all the rocks in the riverbed so I'll be sure to have the one they want." He wasn't kidding. He had a minor kingdom of analysts to sort and polish those measurement rocks.

If leaders chafe under external measurement oversight, they themselves probe extensively in turn. There was a time when I believed that measuring more was the key to staying on top of things. If only I could get reports about XYZ, I would be in control. At best a naive assumption, it was too often a completely wrong one as well. XYZ led to XXyZ, which led to XXYZz in triplicate.

Measures can actually take leaders *off* their game. There is an addictive quality to them that becomes a constant thirst for more detail and precision. That addiction is commonly called micromanaging. Everything begins to look important. The insidious pressure to find the ever more precise measure can supplant other important work. The search for measurement precision can begin to hobble a leader's intuition and strategic perspective.

Measures That Help Everyone *See Better*

By creating such frenzy and cost, measures can sabotage their own purpose and potential. Leaders need a different approach. Using an *interruption* strategy, as I described earlier, leaders can flip some assumptions and open up new possibilities. Here's another illustration for how asking the larger question helps.

Who needs measures? Many leaders see them as a way to peer into their organizations to find out what is going on. That is well and good for the leader, but terribly narrow for the organization. All employees in the organization, not just the leaders, could do better work if they had access to broader and better measures.

Sharing performance measures within organizations is not generally common. The predominant idea is that measures *go up the organization*, not sideways. Leaders are all too often the primary customers for the measures they demand. What about everyone else? A valuable first flip in assumptions involves opening up the span of people with access to measures and engaging them about what they reveal.

Why are we measuring? Too many people trip over this fundamental question. Because leaders want to avoid surprises and get out in front, they are intent on using measures to *sniff out problems*. What if they *welcomed problems* instead?

Changing the purpose of measures could make a world of difference. When leaders use measures apprehensively, they are focusing on history instead of possibility. The question will be "What went wrong?" instead of "What can we learn and adjust?" In response to the former, organizations will spar with their leaders, taking a defensive and protective stance. In response to the latter, an organization is more likely to open up, explore the issues, and partner with the leader on improvements. By engaging an organization in a mutual quest to improve, leaders will find many more wide open and freely sharing avenues in and around the organization.

Leaders are the people who must change the questions. If measures are framed as a *source of insight and possibility for the leader and the entire organization,* they can serve as powerful tools to a healthier, more honest flow of information and knowledge solutions.

Changing the visibility of measures so more can see them and changing the intentions of measures so more can embrace them will increase engagement, build trust, and open up possibilities for improvement. The organization will operate in more light.

Measures That Point Directly toward the Light

On a recent visit to Monticello, I read the logs that Thomas Jefferson famously kept on the weather. He posted the temperature and precipitation twice a day for decades, both when he lived at his estate and when he traveled. He rose very early to take one set of measures at what he assumed to be coldest point of the day. He recorded the other set in the afternoon.

Fascinated by and fastidious about the measures he took, he repeatedly urged others—family, friends, colleagues—to do the same, although no one was as avid and persistent as he. The modern National Weather Service, which currently deploys thousands across the country to monitor, record, analyze, and predict, would be of huge delight and satisfaction to him.

Importantly, Jefferson watched the weather not just because he was something of a data freak, but also because he reckoned that the weather held great power over the pleasures and frustrations of our lives. He of the famous "pursuit of happiness" phrase folded weather conditions into that equation for happiness. He wanted to understand more about the weather so that we could all be *happier.*

To look at his meticulous lists of numbers and his side notes about birds and winds gives one deep respect for this founding father. Jefferson was clearly a man on a mission. He did not simply measure for the sake of measuring. He connected his knowledge about the weather to a much larger social good. He knew exactly why he was measuring.

So should we all.

It is a subtle yet important point. If leaders use measures to probe, organizations can get their backs up. A random searchlight coming from high up does not always encourage people to step forward and wave to be seen.

Instead, measures can be used to illuminate, steer, and connect organizations to the greater good, or the organization's version of Jefferson's goal of happiness. Measures do not stand in isolation. They belong in the line-up of an organization's important work. When used in this manner, leaders truly are taking their organizations toward the light.

Measuring at GSA

As GSA's Administrator, my responsibility was to steer the organization to help the government work better, much better. This was a challenge of the highest order, a truly important point of the horizon. The only way to do this was for the GSA executives to be steering in the same direction with me, intent on taking the agency toward that point on the horizon as well.

How could I help the leadership team do this? How could I use measures to encourage the executives to be united in steering the agency forward?

GSA is assigned about 110 executive slots. For a sprawling organization with over a dozen business lines, this is a reasonable number of executives, and it has held steady for at least two decades. It is, however, a sizeable number for an Administrator to direct. Was there a measure that I could use to support and promote their collective leadership impact?

I did not think that I would find it easily in the executives' performance plans, which were very elaborate and fashioned to comply with federal government policies. While I could ask them to insert a "team element" into their plans, I knew that would compete with other commitments and not carry the power-packed significance required.

As another option, I could ask them to rework their business measures to emphasize how they shared the responsibility for promoting GSA's collective performance. Business measures and their supporting budgets, however, were done by *divisions*—an apt word for the obstacles I was facing in promoting synergies in support of a larger goal.

The answer emerged while posting the executive organization chart up on the wall. By tacking up 110 cards each listing a unique leadership position, it became even more obvious how granulated the team was. Each executive was clearly identified with a box—not with the entire chart. Their titles said so. Their tenure in the positions said so.

The change that would help would be if executives had broader experience around the agency. Staying in one job meant that an executive had a significant challenge to learn, know, and understand GSA as a whole. However, holding different positions and cycling around the organization meant an executive would be less inclined to think and act only in relationship to one job box. He or she would have a larger, agency-wide view.

To assess and encourage this meant measuring job movement among the executives.

I did not have in mind an amount of time that would be the appropriate executive job tenure. I did know, however, that the collective team needed to display movement. My job was to use the measures to make the conversation an important one.

The mechanics were easy. Human Resources gathered tenure information and it was posted on a large bulletin board outside my office. Anyone who came to see me walked past that chart.

It seemed that everyone in the organization knew about that bulletin board. People dropped by simply to see it for themselves. While there was much talk about the fact that Martha Johnson wanted executives to move, there was also a sense that I was demanding something for GSA. This was less about zeroing in on individuals than about demanding a holistic, confident, and flexible leadership *team*. It was important for executives to know more of the whole, not just a piece of it.

This simple measure of executive movement had an effect. While there were individual executives who had previously changed jobs more than the norm, I was thrilled that more of GSA's senior team started to move. Headquarters people moved to regions, staff moved into line positions, and executives moved from one division to another. People crossed expertise boundaries. A real estate expert took a Human Resources position, a finance person went into policy, and so forth. It was a dynamic time. One measure helped nudge the executive team down a collective path for the good of the agency.

There are always tremendous arguments about measures, whether they are input or output measures, calibrated properly, shared effectively, worth the investment, point-specific or trending, aimed at root causes, or indicators. My instinct concerning all of it is to scrutinize the value of measures and de-clutter the measurement activity. The most powerful strategy is to focus on measures *that connect to something important and worth the effort*. In this way, everyone can emerge from the darkness of confusion and see the significant work that needs to be done.

In Conclusion

Yes, the leader will never know it all. There will be shadows, darkness, and clouds. By interrupting old norms and bad habits, being the champion of transparency, and using measures so that everyone can see properly and intelligently, leaders will have the best shot at knowing what they need to know.

CHAPTER TWO
Leading at Scale

Among the many speeches I gave as part of my job at GSA, one stands out. It was in a very large convention center at a meeting on transportation. The room was full of people who worked in the worlds of trains, planes, and automobiles. At about 220,000 vehicles, the GSA fleet was one of the largest in the country. The agency also negotiated the contracts for booking federal travel for millions of trips a year. It was no surprise that I was scheduled to be the opening speaker. Willie Nelson was telling the crowd that he couldn't wait to get on the road again as they ate their enchilada breakfasts.

As I entered the room, I could see that the podium stood in the middle of the stage in front of a huge, I mean gargantuan, screen. I realized I would be standing in front of a live video of my magnified face. Every eyelash would be five feet long.

It would be a new experience to give a speech in front of my own looming image. The proportion was ludicrous, like that massive ocean liner passing right by Tom Hanks on his raft in *Cast Away*. I was a bit put off by the setup, and I was not sure how it would affect the audience as I spoke. Maybe they would not notice, but that was hard to imagine.

After I was introduced to the audience, I stepped up to the podium. I felt the screen bearing down on me from behind. It was too big to ignore, and instinctively I turned to look at it. I was surprised, because of course when I turned, all I saw was the back of my head—four stories of it.

I forced myself to pause to collect my wits. Then I turned back to face the audience and said, "My mother always said a woman should check her hair before giving a speech." There was a split second of dead silence, and then thank heavens, everyone burst out laughing.

Big scale has an effect. It distorts, it disconcerts, and it makes small things huge. It stands right behind us these days, influencing us in ways we do not expect.

Big Is All Around

Bigness is a fact of life for all of us. We are dependent on a world of scale these days: billions of people, massive enterprise, national infrastructure, syndicated news, a blur of options in the grocery store, oceans of traffic, and more. Organizations are consolidating and growing all of the time. More and more leaders are faced with running companies or agencies comparable to small and even medium-sized countries. Leaders find themselves standing at the apex of organizations of huge consequence with masses of people and vast resources.

What does it take to lead massive organizations? How does that work? What is the difference between being the captain of an aircraft carrier and the captain of a sailboat? Both captains have to understand the weather, take care of their craft, and be clear about their directions. So what distinguishes the leadership task when it is about scale?

For one thing, scale means volume. There are lots of locations, tons of names in the directory, oodles of programs, extensive audits, colossal information technology systems, and more. Understanding such quantity and market muscle challenges even the most seasoned of leaders. Size is demanding because it is outside of our day-to-day perspective. When I was at CSC, I was responsible for shifting the organizational culture, which involved 90,000 employees across six continents. When I was at GSA, I reviewed budgets with notations explaining that zeroes were dropped and all numbers were in the thousands or millions. Each situation was voluminous and, therefore, formidable.

For another thing, scale magnifies even the inconsequential. My every eyelash and wrinkle could be seen on the Jumbo-

Tron. Likewise, a minor adjustment in technology, reimbursements, work hours, or any other routine matter ripples for a great distance in a large organization. A slight shift can vastly increase the possibility for unintended consequences. It is like living in a sci-fi movie in which the bugs become dragons and the dust becomes boulders. Small becomes big.

In order to deal with both volume and the magnification of the inconsequential, leaders need strategic *proportion*. They need to lead with an eye to strategic scale. The sections ahead lay out two ideas for doing this. The first is to hold fast to the view of the horizon. The second is to design deliberately for vast quantities and repetition.

Leading at the *Right* Scale: The Horizon View

Taking the large and long view is the job of a leader and it is not easy. At least three forces can bear down on leaders and pull them away from holding the horizon view.

The first is a purely human reaction to the outsized tasks and responsibilities at hand and calls out the instinct to protect oneself.

Two years ago, my husband and I drove from Aspen to Colorado Springs, up and over Independence Pass. It is a fabulous drive full of scenery and a winding road up and up and up, and then down and down and down over the Rocky Mountains.

As beautiful as it was, I always find that kind of driving demanding. On road trips I like to watch the scenery and turn to my husband to make eye contact as we talk. However, on that steep Route 82, I was all focus and discipline. I had to keep my eyes hard on the road. It was not a time to gaze around or try spotting the stream at the bottom of the drop-off.

When we finally made it to the top, we got out of the car to stretch our legs. The view was spectacular and well worth the effort. We could see for miles, since we were above the tree line. Strolling in a large circle, we could feel the vastness of the Rocky

Mountains stretching in every direction. The sky was the palest of blues, and various peaks in the distance were white with snow.

Getting chilly, we returned to the car and rummaged around for jackets. I continued by fussing with others items—stacking pillows, moving the cooler, and securing magazines that were slipping around in the back seat. It was comforting in a strange way. The enormous vista felt overwhelming. I was disoriented and almost dizzy from looking at such distances. I was happy to remain in the car and leave the scenery to itself.

Vast panoramas of scenery can dwarf a person. The geology of time, the spread of the view, and the change in the air remind us of large forces beyond our own human scale. They distort our sense of distance, temperature, and time. Turning to something close at hand and mundane is a normal way to balance things out.

Leading at scale is not very different. Vast organizations need leaders to step into a special large dimension. Only a handful of people, if not just one at the top of the hierarchy, are properly positioned to see both across the full organization and out to markets and society. It falls to the leader to stay true to that perspective, look to the horizon, scan for macro shifts in the economy and society, and incorporate the large movements in demand, resources, and talent.

It is, however, easy to turn our attention to small things. It is a human reaction. We all feel the urge to straighten the metaphorical backseat of the car. It is a natural, if not well-practiced, instinct to work on what is right in front of you. When the world seems to spin, people gain balance by looking right down at their own feet. We have all shared the feeling that getting our desks cleared or the dishes washed would be a huge step forward for humankind. For leaders at scale, this natural inclination crowds out the crucial work of scanning the horizon.

The second force that pushes on a leader to compromise the horizon view is about skill. Truth be told, there are few places to learn to be confident and comfortable leading vastness.

Part of the challenge is that people usually become leaders by maturing through various jobs and levels in a system. While leadership development can include experience at a division or large group level, it is when leaders ascend the tops of their organizations that they face the full scope, the 360-degree circle of view and responsibilities.

Once there, it seems counterintuitive to leave behind sometimes well-honed habits of the previous roles. *The work that leads a person to leadership, however, is not necessarily the work of leadership.*

To step into the strategic role and focus on the horizon is a tougher switch to make than many might imagine. It requires a form of abandonment. Many of the skills, behaviors, and habits of the past, which seemingly paved the way into leadership, now must be shelved. Letting go of logistics, schedules, step-by-step improvement plans, and so on, seems wrong.

A leader might also simply like the old routines and activities and actually miss them. I know the impulse. I still enjoy the mental game of developing Excel spreadsheets and the soothing (for me) process of cleaning out my files. The previous partial or granulated view no longer serves when the job is about the horizon view. Yet it is difficult to grasp that what worked for so long is not core to success leading at scale.

Finally, the third force that pulls leaders away from the horizon view is none other than their own institutions. Organizations yammer at leaders for input and specific direction. Too often employees want concrete instructions, and petitioners wait for a chance to make their plea for particular attention.

As Administrator, I couldn't get on the elevator without someone lobbying me about any number of issues that belonged elsewhere. I was asked to decree uniform office space limits, order employees not to use the "Reply All" button on emails, review nominees for training courses, and on and on. The minnows are ever ready to nibble a leader to death.

Strategic leadership means *holding tight to the right role.* No one else is positioned or accountable for taking the system-wide perspective. Leaders who are responsible for organizations of heft and scale have to lift their heads and get out the binoculars. Their entire visual frame has to change.

Leadership Practices for Handling Scale

Leaders at scale must learn to be comfortable with the vertigo from standing on deck, so to speak, while the ocean vessel is shifting under foot. The small waves go undetected. The big waves matter and require a leader to stay vertical, avoid dizziness, and find new ways of moving effectively.

I found a handful of simple practices helped me gain those sea legs. Each is a habit of the mind that keeps things in balance and the proper order.

A first practice is to screen an idea to see if it is a priority by asking the simple question, "Why bother?" This is a request for the arguments and rationale to justify placing the enterprise's vast resources, energy, or even reputation on an issue. This is a case-building technique that lays out the value of a priority. If the scenario turns out to be paltry or hesitant, the leader can shift promptly to the larger and bigger issues that match the right strategic perspective.

A second practice is to confirm a priority by asking "Why?" five times. Given the distortions that a leader faces when working at scale, it is useful to have simple ways to confirm that, indeed, the matter at hand rises to the right level of importance.

Q: Why is this important?
A:
Q: Dig a little more. Why is that important?
A:
Q: And now tell me why that is important.
A:
Q: And again, why is that important?
A:

Q: I have one last question: why is that important?

A:

Going through the sequence is surprisingly tough. As early as the second question, it is often already apparent whether an issue has legs. By the third "why," it usually is clear whether the issue is a keeper or not.

The third practice is to organize the work so priorities are always clear. At first blush this does not sound like unique advice. Middle school students probably get a lecture about managing their priorities in every homeroom class. For leaders at scale, however, the challenge is often about clarifying priorities for an organization, because size and consequence can be so distorting.

The basic principle is that the A Work, or the big wave, gets attention; the B Work gets a nod and is assigned elsewhere; and the C Work is put aside.

A colleague once brought some props to a training session in order to make the differences clear. He had an empty bucket, a pile of rocks, a pile of gravel, and a third pile of sand. All three piles needed to be loaded in the bucket. The point was obvious before he started. If you load in the rocks first, the gravel fits around it, and the sand filters into the remaining space. If you start with the sand, things will not fit. So start with the Big Stuff, the A Work.

When leading at scale, it should be noted, the C Work can seem like A Work simply because its dimensions can be sizeable. To the normal eye, C Work appears to be Big Stuff. Leaders have to recalibrate.

At GSA I could not delve deeply into each of the working units, even though they amounted individually to the size of significant corporations. While the fleet division managed 220,000 vehicles and the real estate division was launching the second largest building project in the government (headquarters for the Department of Homeland Security), my position was as the head of the whole shebang. My A Work was to be sure the leadership of those divisions was the best talent available and that they had the resources and support to do their jobs.

Whatever it takes, a leader needs to keep an eye on the right ball. When big and BIG can both be well beyond normal human scale, a leader should not hesitate to use whatever devices necessary to handle a scaled and strategic perspective.

Leading at the *Right* Scale: Design for a Million

We have all played the word game that asks you to blurt out your first thoughts upon hearing a phrase. If I were to say, "lead massive institutions," you would probably respond with phrases such as "large deals," "big risk," "tons of money," "media management," "many employees," "stock market," or "global markets." I would be surprised if your first responses zeroed in on "design."

I believe a significant difference in leading at scale involves design, that is, creative adjustments to the way things are done. Big organizations do a lot of something. Many are shaping or manipulating big volumes of material or product in a process that is repeated over and over and over again.

Think of companies that build computers, churn out plastic bottles, sell gas, or serve billions of hamburgers. Think of government organizations that handle tax returns, issue drivers' licenses, or process visas. Over and over, a work process is repeated item after item after item, or transaction after transaction after transaction.

Big organizations also function at a massive volume in and of themselves: in their meetings, reporting, reviews, communications, space, technology, buying, travel, and much more. Inside big organizations people make the same decisions, take the same actions, and follow the same patterns, over and over and over.

Explicit design leadership is a necessity when an organization does the same thing repeatedly *at scale*. Design, in this case, is the ability to construct a product or a process as intelligently as possible, so that when it is produced or repeated a million times, there are absolutely no unnecessary loops or parts.

I am currently making a wedding quilt. It is a Travel-around-the-World pattern with hundreds of 2.5" square blocks of cloth. Exactness matters. If the template for those squares is off by a 16th of an inch, I will cut the hundreds of pieces slightly wrong, and they will not fit together neatly. My blanket will be skewed. The blue batik material has to be cut into *exactly* 2.5" squares. I have been careful to check my cutting board, straighten the weave of the material, and measure twice before cutting. In other words, getting it right involves exact equipment, procedure, and material. No detail is too small, especially when it is to be repeated 800 times.

Making a quilt, like running a big organization, is about finding the bits that are repetitive and carefully studying and improving on them. The smallest decisions and choices, if repeated endlessly and into the future, can make a huge difference.

The leader's job is to forge the way to better design. The leader must inspire and steer the organization in this direction. A design culture must become a strategic goal that includes building and resourcing a capability for asking design questions, thinking from different angles and perspectives, analyzing detail, and making constant upgrades. What is the purpose of this work or task? Is each part of the process necessary? Are steps taken in the best sequence? What embellishments occur? Where are mistakes cropping up?

A leader needs to think about design in an *explosive* way. Remember Mickey Mouse as the sorcerer's apprentice in the movie, *Fantasia*? The brooms keep multiplying and carrying more and more buckets of water. Eventually the situation overwhelms Mickey. Leaders of scaled situations need to think about an explosion of brooms and buckets. They need to encourage design as if every product or process exploded, so to speak, multiplying a zillion times.

Simultaneously, a leader must appreciate and encourage the need to think in extremely minute, even infinitesimal detail. This might seem to fly in the face of my earlier exhortation to work on A Work, also known as the Big Stuff. However, *better design is the Big Stuff*. Nothing is too small, particularly considering the consequences when something small is multiplied for scale.

A leader does not *do* the work of design. The leader's job is to make it a priority. The organizational strategy and culture must be framed with design at the forefront. Educating everyone so that many eyes and ears are looking for opportunities to improve is high on the list.

A good designer is a precious talent to be trained or recruited and nurtured. Some of the most effective experts are those trained in business process re-engineering, which involves studying and redesigning processes for maximum efficiency and effectiveness.

The brilliance of a design strategy is that it can engage every single person in the organization. Everyone has experience and thoughts about how things could be better designed. Once ideas are invited and they contribute to improvements, many more ideas will surface. Potential for design improvement exists everywhere: in mechanics, construction process, functionality, sequencing, and any number of other areas.

When my father retired, he took a seasonal job in the state tax office reviewing tax returns. He told me that one worker had the assignment of taking staples out of the incoming packets. Other people took the loose forms, copied them, and then stapled them back together. Dad thought this was an example of a bureaucracy being absolutely daft.

To me, this stapling process sounded like bad design. The stapling cycle meant wasted time, tedious effort, and unnecessary rework. Done five or ten times, a person might ignore it and perhaps laugh about it. Repeated thousands of times, it adds up to noticeable inefficiency, tedium, and possibly even carpal tunnel syndrome.

There are many ways to apply design to improve things in this situation. My father could see the problem. Others surely could as well. If the managers in the office made it clear that they considered efficiency improvements a priority, I have no doubt my father would have pointed this one out. At the simplest levels, people in the office could have been solicited for ideas to smooth the process. A business process reengineering expert added to the mix could introduce techniques for brainstorming and implementing solutions.

GSA was well-supplied with arenas ripe for design-for-scale. For starters, we were obsessive about efficiently managing the 220,000 vehicles in the fleet and sought to design information systems that could hint at opportunities for savings. We tracked gas usage through charge cards, clocked travel patterns, watched maintenance schedules, and analyzed vehicle performance to find new efficiencies.

In our travel business, we were able to mine the data from the 10 million trips taken every year by government employees. Analysis could explain the impact of luggage, weight, and seating choices on fuel efficiency. The team found better routes, suggested better meeting destinations, and linked air tickets and ground travel for better package deals.

GSA staff could help federal departments analyze their travel patterns and set better localized policies. They were able to tell, for example, the number and types of trips that had been scheduled at the last minute and therefore cost more. Constantly improving the design of travel policies with these insights saved the government enormous amounts of money and time.

GSA's vast real estate inventory also offered a special design-for-scale opportunity. The property managers surveyed, identified, and studied ways to improve building operations. Then they could pass around a cost-saving trick, a safer product, or a better practice that would improve the functioning of the entire inventory of buildings. Because it was such a large portfolio of buildings, a change that worked in one could be deployed at scale across all.

Additionally, the portfolio of buildings was spread across the nation and, therefore, sat in almost every climate and altitude imaginable. It was a tremendous test bed for innovations that helped improve energy consumption.

For example, the Green Proving Ground program tried out various designs for solar panels, sensing equipment, and building controls. The agency studied and then switched to green cleaning products in building maintenance contracts. Staff eked out large savings by installing software to turn computers off at night automatically and by using motion sensors to control lights. Small improvements had energy efficiency impact by virtue of the massive government footprint of real estate. They could also be picked up and put into broader commercial usage. What great leverage!

In a vast organization, design competence supports improvement in even the most mundane tasks such as paying benefits, ordering supplies, filing papers, punching time clocks, or greeting visitors. The time, materials, space, resources, or commodities involved are small in the single instance. One group holding an inefficient meeting is just that—some wasted time spread across a group of people. Multiplied across thousands of instances and tens of thousands of people, better meeting design can yield a huge value.

In Conclusion

Organizations at scale pose particular challenges to leaders. On the one hand, a leader's *own behaviors* have to adjust to the unusual horizon view from their position. On the other hand, leaders can support a design strategy and culture in which organizations take on the *habits of design*—digging for and improving every value angle. The right perspective and the right design, particularly at scale, matter.

CHAPTER THREE
Leading under Oath

I am going to switch gears for one chapter to focus exclusively on the challenges of government leadership. I do so because I believe there are public sector leadership stories that have meaning for all. I know that when government leaders find creative solutions, they do so under very difficult circumstances. They should be applauded, but more importantly, they should be studied, for they have unraveled tough knots.

The contract for my position as Administrator at GSA read:

> *I, Martha Johnson, do solemnly swear that I will support and defend the Constitution of the United States against all enemies, foreign and domestic; that I will bear true faith and allegiance to the same; that I take this obligation freely, without any mental reservation or purpose of evasion; and that I will well and faithfully discharge the duties of the office on which I am about to enter. So help me God.*

Each person entering the federal government takes this Oath of Office. One of the privileges of my job was to administer the Oath of Office at times to new employees. During this brief swearing-in ceremony, I have seen people raise their right hands, speak these words, and weep. The Oath of Office, though short and concise, is a powerful tie between an individual and a larger effort on behalf of the nation. It speaks to the deepest of our shared hopes for our country.

It sure does not give a lot of specifics about the job, however.

This chapter starts with some discussion of the way in which a public sector job differs from one in the private sector. It then moves on to surface three of the biggest challenges of government assignments and to suggest ways to steer through them.

What I Faced and What I Relied On

Leading under oath was a tough ballgame. At GSA I found myself working in a maze and haze of difficulties.

Some were similar to my private sector experiences, while others were unique. I had to operate under the overhang of history and a we-have-already-tried-that attitude. The surround sound of laws and regulations narrowed my options and agility. I was prepared for the government to be monolithic and impersonal, but the agency was a more pixilated picture, where the real problem was connecting multiple missions and cultures coherently. To top it off, I encountered an insidious culture war between a "rights" government and a "performance" government.

I could not be passive in the face of these problems. Being hogtied is no excuse for giving up. The core challenge—change or die—was not new. The twenty-first century promises no easy security anywhere, and the stakes were, and arc, steadily increasing. Government is in the crosshairs, widely and loudly criticized as inefficient and ineffective. There is pressure to cut it to the bone. Like all public sector leaders, I was under the gun. Hedging and keeping the powder dry were not options.

GSA's issues were heavyweight ones. The real estate folks were battling energy costs and adjusting to the effects of the mortgage-sparked Great Recession. The information technology teams were facing big, one-of-a-kind government legacy systems (for example, taxes, Social Security payments, weather monitoring) while the market was moving into an increasingly disaggregated delivery mode (everyone carrying devices). Cyber security compounded our headaches into migraines. The travel division was coping with contractors such as the airlines struggling with huge capital commitments, rising fuel costs, and industry consolidations.

Government leaders need attitude, a stubbornness, and moxie. I also needed jiu-jitsu. The tighter the constraints, the more I needed different leverage, flexibility, and powerful gymnastic moves. For me this meant emphasizing innovation. I was lucky it was in my bones. I had built up my creative marrow in great assignments over my career:

Company	Innovation Lessons
Ben & Jerry's	Originality in corporate culture, use of theater arts, and brand management
CSC (Computer Sciences Corporation)	Crowd-sourcing, ideation
SRA–Touchstone Consulting Group	Meeting designs that spark strategic thinking, creative work culture encouraged by creative workspace
Cummins Engine Company	Overhauling a system lickety-split

I knew transformation could occur. I believed—and still do—that the massive fight in our society about the role of government (should it be big, small, bashed, supported, loved, hated, feared, adored) would shift and diminish if the government itself performed better. I understood GSA's strategic role: our organization's *mission* was to help government work better. We were at the *epicenter* of what needed to change. I had a job to do, and I knew what it was.

The Terms of the Job

It is not easy to get into government. Available jobs are hard to identify, and the application process is a constant challenge both to applicants and the government itself. Whether applying as a new hire, running for office, or waiting for a political appointment, the job of getting a job in government is arduous. Yes, government employees hang on tenaciously to their jobs. That hardly seems irrational to me, considering that getting the job in the first place is no walk in the park.

Curiously, government work means opposite things to subsets of its employees. For career civil servants, a government job is considered solid and stable. There are many protections for government workers that create a certain level of predictability and job security. While holding on to their government jobs is not an absolute promise, it is a much more reliable assumption than for workers in the private sector. Businesses are subjected to erratic shifts as they respond to market dynamics and financial deals, both of which cause realignments, mergers, and layoffs. Job changing and job loss are inevitable.

Meanwhile, in government, elected and appointed officials comprise a second subset of employees, who face tremendous job *insecurity*. They hold their jobs by virtue of elections and have little by way of protections. The only certainty in their job security is the ticking of the election cycle. As a result, this group carries a strong sense of imperative, urgency, and pacing. In this they work under a reality different from their colleagues, the career civil servants.

I was no different in terms of securing my government job; it was a long and difficult process. To become the Administrator of GSA, first I had to complete financial and security paperwork. It took about a month of long evenings to gather and record the information properly, with many emails to the government lawyers to clarify issues. (Please understand that I am neither wealthy nor engulfed in legal problems. I was a straightforward candidate, with nothing particularly unusual about my record. If anything, I was fairly routine and boring.)

Next I spent hours in various security interviews with the FBI and with lawyers from the White House. The questions ranged from the tedious to the laughable to the truly invasive. "Is this the complete list of people you met on your trip to London in 1984?" "Have you ever conspired to overthrow the government?" "Is there anything about you that would embarrass the President?" "How is your relationship with your husband?"

Then I had to prepare for my confirmation hearings before the United States Senate. I covered the walls and windows of my dining room with big sheets of paper that listed the top 100 questions I expected to be asked. I stood in the middle of the room for hours, turning from chart to chart and practicing my responses.

My next task was to pay courtesy calls on certain senators on the committee that would vote to send my nomination to the full Senate. When the hearing day finally came, I put on a dark suit and herded friends and family to the event.

Once the June 3, 2009, Senate hearing was over, I waited first for the committee and then the full Senate to vote on my confirmation. Unfortunately, my nomination was caught up in the all-too-common need now in the politics of the Senate for a cloture vote in the face of a lone Senator putting a hold on a candidate. In my case, the hold involved Senator Bond, a Republican from Missouri, and his demands over plans for federal buildings in Kansas City. The White House is not in the habit of making real estate deals in order to entice confirmation votes, so my nomination languished.

The lost time hurt in more ways than one. GSA had been without a confirmed Administrator for years and the delay further compromised its clarity of strategy and direction. Personally, I was particularly saddened that my mother did not live to see me raise my hand and take the Oath of Office. She died in September.

Luckily, I continued to work at CSC, which was very gracious about keeping me focused, busy, and productive. Friends and family watched a lot of C-SPAN to see if things were progressing. When the vote was finally cast on February 4, 2010, it was unanimous (96–0), thus demonstrating that the politics of delay had not been about me personally.

In some ironic way, the long and difficult preparation for public service is itself a screening process. Passing the first hurdle gives a sense of the stamina required for other obstacles that the bureaucracy can kick up. Each one of them—and there were many—exacts paperwork, patience, persistence, political skill, and prayer.

Taking the oath, as brief as it is, puts a person under a huge obligation. The responsibilities it engenders are like fireworks which light up in every direction: up, down, and across. The commitment differs significantly from that required of a leadership role in the private sector. Therein lie considerable nuance and context that a person must master immediately.

The task at hand is to lead an organization, program, or commission. Any experienced manager has a sense of the job, which involves steering people and resources to fulfill the mission and is the kind of work widely discussed in business curriculum and literature. The job is complicated, but not mysterious. Leaders understand the responsibility to manage "down" the organization, "up" to boards, "out" to customers, and the like.

For political appointees, the web of responsibility has special characteristics. Once the President is elected, he or she must choose a team. Those accepting an offer of an appointment serve *at the pleasure of the President.*

Each person who signs on occupies a box, referred to as The Office, in the government's organizational chart. Each Office is also part of the cadre called The Administration. I hesitate to call it a team, because it includes hundreds, if not thousands, of people and is much too big for conventional work relationships or even the possibility of knowing everyone.

Appointees technically report up to the President and are responsible for staff down in their respective organization. They have a strong mutual obligation to each other across the Administration, however. It was not unusual to receive a call from an appointee whom I had never met and who was in a completely different part of the government. In the course of the conversation, little was said in terms of pleasantries. Mostly it was a rapid-fire exchange about the business at hand.

"Let me brief you on the problem we've got."

"Sure, I'm listening. How can I help?"

Corporate CEOs do not have this type of relationship. They do not have hundreds of colleagues with whom they share a general mission. There is little in the way of shared obligation to CEOs of other companies in their industry. They might have social networks or business relationships, but not mutual, supportive, collegial *responsibilities.*

This was a particularly crucial part of my role at GSA, because we served the whole of government, the very organizations that my Administration colleagues led. They were both my colleagues and my customers.

One other wrinkle separates those who lead under oath: the President is the boss. I held my positions in government, as did other political appointees, because President Clinton and then President Obama held theirs. I received a salary, invitations to various White House social events, and the opportunity to share in the workings of federal power as afforded by law.

I also, importantly, had responsibilities. I was expected to be in alignment with the White House, be part of the team, and support the directions and policies that the President set. My job was to be loyal to the President and his administration. Such loyalty in the present political culture, however, is not necessarily reciprocated.

In the old days, it worked a bit differently. A patronage system, often the early culture in local and national government, meant that political leaders, also known as bosses, created a culture of loyalty. The officials doled out jobs and favors in order to get votes and support. The political machine made sure that immigrants were met with food, coffee, information, and welcome as they debarked from their ships. Political bosses invested in constituents (loyalty downward) in order to secure their votes and, by extension, the votes of their families and clans (loyalty upward). It was a two-way street.

Today the loyalty equation has frayed. Loyalty still flows up the political ladder, but it does not readily flow down. Political bosses do not rely on a calculus that connects jobs and favors to votes. Besides, with political patronage reforms, only a handful of jobs can be handed out. In addition, the expanding franchise of the last century has commoditized voters. Political parties are different animals. The world of politics has evolved.

In my case, the GSA Western Regions' Training Conference in Las Vegas served up a scandal that became a source of criticism of the Administration during an election year, and, therefore, a potential political liability. It was my role to be loyal to the President. To prevent the liability from spreading, I took the hit. I did not seriously protest, stall, or game it.

Before my last meeting with the White House, I had hoped to negotiate actions to be taken regarding two senior political appointees with shared oversight of the executive in charge of the Las Vegas conference. The White House position was clear that the two appointees were not to be allowed to resign. They were to be fired.

The severity of the decision reflected the extent of the perceived liability that the scandal had created. In the wake of that perception, the option of my resignation was no longer speculative. The potential political damage of the conference story reflected brightly upon me and had to stop there.

CEOs might resign to defend their decisions or their organizations. They do not, however, tend to resign in order to support someone on their Board of Directors. Government appointees have more points of responsibility on their compasses.

⌒

Leading under oath requires certain particular commitments and responsibilities that are directly connected to the demands of public service. Many dilemmas that government leaders face, however, are not very different from those experienced by leaders in other types of organizations. I have chosen three that I encountered both while I was in office and in the private sector:

tight rules and constraints, claustrophobic history, and the risky side of organizational culture.

Ignoring these dilemmas is not wise. Doing battle with them is also a misuse of energy. Each dilemma offers a power and force that leaders can use as a platform for reaching a new level of effectiveness. By facing each dilemma, leaders can find new handles for leverage or different ways to direct the energy. Thus a leader can find ways to squeeze out innovation, to choose and leverage historic stories that can motivate an organization, and to invest more seriously in understanding and managing cultural risk.

The thoughts I share here are not about sugar coating or turning lemons into lemonade. They are about creative leadership that never loses as chance to *reconfigure or redeem* tough circumstances. In addition, public sector leaders work in a setting flooded with difficulties. Stories about their progress can benefit and sharpen the thinking of *all* our nation's leaders.

Leading by *Facing* Constraints

I came to my job as Administrator of GSA with a briefcase full of experience. Like many other people who arrive in government from the outside, I was primed to bring my perspectives. I knew all about organizational inefficiency, process problems, resource shortages, and the difficulties in getting people to change. I was sure I knew how to get the government running better. My mindset was not unusual. I believe that making a difference is a nearly universal desire of people entering public service.

Quickly, however, the walls seemed to move closer, shrinking the size of the room. A number of particular constraints soon limited my scope and movement.

The first was that *my team was not all mine*. I knew that change makers can't do it alone. The rule is that the individual crusader model rarely works. Instead, change makers must have *compadres*. I was quite excited that some extraordinary professionals agreed to join me at GSA. However, building the full team was not entirely my own choice. Political expediency and larger

Administration needs meant there were others less experienced at strategic change for big systems who found their way onto the GSA leadership team.

The second was that *change was dictated by law.* This is fundamental to government. Through legislation, Congress has the power to change an organization's mandate, reconfigure its organizational chart, redistribute its budget, and demand reports. Inevitably, the core rationale for change becomes "They told us to."

What if a government leader wants other change? What about improving performance, upgrading security, or building new relationships with the public? If the overriding norm of the organization is based in law, how does a leader convince the organization to change, short of getting a bill through Congress?

I do not know about others, but I can rarely get people (employees, colleagues, husband, kids!) to change simply *because I tell them to.* The rule of law requires an environment of respect for the law, but it adds a sense of rigidity about how change occurs. It also dilutes a leader's options for motivating change.

Business leaders can build a more flexible and immediate imperative for change by using the arguments of a business case. They can bring new evidence and motivate people with emerging opportunities. "We need to change because the markets are shifting." "The recession is creating a gap." "The demand for this product is growing." These messages differ vastly from "Congress ordered it, the President signed it, and that is what we adhere to."

To show how this plays out, take the example of the Clinger-Cohen Act of 1996 and other acquisition reform law around the same time that dramatically adjusted GSA's mandate. Those laws revamped much of GSA's mission and a number of its specific assignments.

The Clinger-Cohen Act made government agencies more directly responsible for their information technology buying and management, a role that in many ways GSA had shouldered previously. The laws directed GSA to abandon much of its company-store-for-the-government mandate and work more directly in response to the pressures of the market.

GSA in this new incarnation was to be supplier of choice. That meant government customers could decide to buy through GSA or could go directly to businesses to procure their goods and services. All in all, these were good laws that set GSA in a more dynamic market environment and caused it to abandon dated business models that did not maximize possibilities for the best price, good quality, or efficiency.

To handle the new laws, GSA had to learn to compete, deliver, and perform in new ways. Divisions within GSA were abolished, and other organizations had to be reconfigured. Jobs changed, and people had to move. The new laws did not spell out many details, of course, and like many other aspects of mandated change, new policy had to be developed to tell people what they could and could not do.

All that guidance presents a conflicting invitation for change to employees. Do they wait to be told to change? Can they change here or there without guidance? I find it stunning that there is any appetite for change in the government, cloaked as it is with so much guidance. I also was confirmed in my belief that the levers I had for innovation and change were to be found in cultural and behavioral arenas, since structure and resources were so predetermined.

The third constraint was that *oversight was ferocious*. Along with conforming to the new laws, GSA had to work in an environment rife with oversight:

- The media
- The Freedom of Information Act
- Whistleblowers under the Whistleblower Protection Act
- The General Accountability Office
- Ethics law, as well as guidance and review by the White House Office of Government Ethics
- Inspectors General

- Congressional oversight committees
- Executive hiring approval panels at the Office of Personnel Management
- Appeals boards, such as the Federal Labor Relations Authority and the Merit Systems Protection Board.

Like other government leaders, I often felt I was expected to move mountains, as demanded by Congress, but my work boots were cemented to the stones on the path to the mountain.

The fourth was that *any move complicated other moves*. Organizations do not usually jump for joy about changing. In government the normal reluctance around change was further complicated, because anything done might tear at the web of rules around us. As a result, I did very little without a lawyer next to me or nearby. People trained in the law filled a number of senior staff positions, as well as operations or line management positions reporting to me. I had to learn to think about management decisions through legal lenses. It was not easy.

The fifth was that *the clock has its own rhythm*. Government organizations are ruled by a peculiar clock. The rhythm of the schedule is dictated by elections and the budget year. It is a fixed meter, not the explosions of tempo in business caused by swings in the market, interest rates, or sudden changes in taste. The government cycle of activity has a steady heartbeat and there is little to be done to speed up the pulse. I found that change was not easily hurried.

To sum it up, I was trussed up and hemmed in, running a three-legged race. Law, calendars, organizational reluctance, bureaucratic permafrost, and a rather uneven team around me provided a combo of constraints. It was like an MRI enclosure, tight and narrow.

I had a choice. On the one hand, I could whine about the boundaries and lament the loss of elbowroom. But little is served by complaining. It is dispiriting and, coming from the leader, it sends a depressing message to everyone else. What kind of leader does that?

On the other hand, I could resort to jiu-jitsu. *Face* the constraints and find what there was to *love* and leverage about them. Trust they were there in order to spur creativity and innovation. Bring it on! GSA's response would be to out-innovate, over-imagine, feed the creative beast in us, and find the ingenious. We could not just be clever; we would be damn clever.

I did not delay. In my opening speech to employees, I said I was not interested in complicated models or big theories. I was interested in promoting three priorities: customer intimacy to secure our markets; operational excellence to secure our performance; and, for our future, "Let's innovate our hearts out."

GSA made tracks and I did my level best to be out front promoting our innovation agenda. I tried any number of angles, including:

- *Claiming innovation in our strategy.* I started by embracing a strategy to place GSA in the middle of government innovation. The agency was a membrane between the private sector and government. It was a unique place and opportunity to link the innovative progress of the former to the latter.

- *Profiling best practices.* I met with and toured both high and low profile innovative companies: a car battery recycling business that had designed and fabricated much of its capital equipment itself, green architects, solar panel manufacturers, Google, OnStar, Enterprise Cars, and dozens more.

- *Demonstrating flexibility.* I personally made a dramatic office move from the Administrator's historic office space to a cubicle. GSA's headquarters at 1800 F Street in Washington, D.C., dated back to 1917. Reaching across a wing of the building, my office was one of the largest in the capital. It boasted wood paneling, a fireplace, beveled glass windows, a secret closet, and chandeliers. In a swing-space building where we moved during a renovation, however, I took a cubicle that was about 8' by 8'. All I really needed was an American flag and reliable technology, and I was in business.

- *Taking risks.* I jumped on new technologies, urged GSA (and the government) into the cloud, used various mobile devices, employed social networking tools, and personally wrote documents collaboratively.

- *Challenging convention.* I eschewed the conventional big black Crown Victoria government car and drove a small gray hybrid. I teased other departmental leaders that if they were concerned about security, they might try a less conspicuous option. Besides, I always found parking spaces.

- And much more.

Each activity helped build a stronger culture of innovation and soon signs of that were appearing across the GSA organization. Regional offices started to adjust their own workspaces for flexibility and energy savings. Communities of practice proliferated allowing employees to share ideas and best practices. Other government agencies took note of our new liveliness, requested tours of our space, invited us to speak at their meetings, and welcomed our ideas and examples of technology tools.

Frankly, all government works in a setting that is like a very tightly woven rope. To support all of its customers and be effective itself, GSA was obligated to twist the rope carefully and systematically *against the weave* until some new light, new ideas, new options could be seen through the threads. We had to be creative *so that* the entire government could find new energy and possibility for change as well.

Leading by *Facing* History

Rarely does a leader in the private sector exist inside the dusty library of history in quite the same way that a government leader does. Some agencies such as the Census Bureau and Patent and Trademark Office are anchored in the Constitution itself. GSA is over 60 years old, a relative youngster. Its headquarters are located a block from the White House in the building that originally housed the Department of the Interior. My historic office had been the scene of the bribe payment that touched off the Teapot Dome Scandal in the 1920s. The molding above the fireplace harkened back to townhouses in medieval London.

Longevity is the name of the game. It is everywhere. Very old laws governed us. One of my favorites was the Heights of Buildings Act of 1910, which limits the height of a building in Washington, D.C., to the width of the street on which it sits.

Many federal workers spend their entire careers in one organization, creating a solid layer of historical institutional memory. Lawyers at GSA, for example, could recite legal decisions and case histories from decades past. Building managers remembered construction projects that were now old enough to need renovation.

For all of its colorful and informative aspects, history is too often used within bureaucracy to block change. I wish I had airline points for all of the times I heard, "We used to do it that way, but it didn't work so well." Those wet blanket comments easily extinguish any enthusiasm or energy available for finding good solutions. As a leader, I did not need history thrown at me—I needed history to be my buddy.

It can be a friend, and a powerful one. Here is one particularly spectacular story from GSA's timeline. In the 1960s and 1970s, the agency was, of course, responsible for constructing and managing federal buildings, but the pressures, expectations, and contracting requirements at the time drove decisions to keep costs at bedrock bottom. GSA stayed within those constraints, and therefore we have a gloomy heritage of low-cost buildings from that period. The buildings show minimal creativity or imagination; they look bleak and sterile; and the work environments they house are depressing.

Starting in the late 1970s, GSA began to shape a new way of designing federal buildings. Referencing principles about government architecture and physical structures crafted by Senator Daniel Patrick Moynihan in the 1960s, GSA's Chief Architect and others laid the foundation of the Design Excellence program that was officially launched in the 1990s. The program emphasizes creativity, includes a competitive process for selecting the design and engineering team, and uses private-sector peers for feedback.

The architecture, design, and engineering professions responded enthusiastically. Government buildings are substantial structures, visible to the public, and filled with potential for important statements about their democratic function. They are an architect's dream for showcasing the best of the profession. Federal building projects offer prestige and longevity, designed as they are for the long haul as sites for dispensing justice and services well into the future.

Under Design Excellence, GSA's new construction began to exhibit interesting and beautiful placement and design, innovative energy features, and new dignity. With a relatively small investment for critically acclaimed architecture, the federal building landscape started to change.

Federal buildings began to win design awards and were soon gracing the front pages of prestigious architectural and construction magazines. Visitors and those who worked in the buildings were able to appreciate and understand public service better. New federal buildings have become, again, remarkable statements of our shared democratic ideals. Americans visiting the Design Excellence buildings (http://www.gsa.gov/portal/category/21079) find that their spirits lift, their pride increases, and their sense of the possible is expanded.

The story of the Design Excellence program was a very important part of the organization's history because GSA had effectively turned on a dime. The agency had demonstrated the imagination and capability to transform something that had been a visible and national disappointment. The organization could point to powerful, amazing, and important results. I could call on that organizational DNA to encourage our imagination and reassure myself that asking for big changes was neither unrealistic nor fantastical.

The Design Excellence story was not GSA's only phoenix story. In the 1990s GSA jumped early into the online ordering of products, rapidly changing the entire experience of government purchasing. Goods could be called up quickly on the screen and much more easily displayed. Buyers could conveniently comparison shop.

In many ways, GSA was ahead of the private sector in envisioning dramatically new ways to buy, sell, and dispose of goods. Online auctions and reverse auctions were two highly successful innovations set up by GSA teams in those years.

GSA also set new levels of innovation for the government at large with its early and widespread use of the internet. Administrator Dave Barram challenged the organization in the spring of 1996 to assure that the internet was available to every employee... by Flag Day. Not only was the technology a major boost to GSA's capability and reputation, it also was a boost in learning rapid implementation.

History gave me some important indications about GSA's potential for almost radical creativity. I never felt I was asking too much when I pushed the organization to modernize, change, and innovate. One can believe in the power of human potential, but in the grind of everyday bureaucratic life it sure helped to know that I did not need to convince GSA that things were possible; I just needed to remind them of what they already knew.

Leading by *Facing* Culture

If leaders can benefit from understanding organizational history, they also must pay close attention to organizational culture. I return repeatedly to the issue of culture, for it is in so many ways the least leveraged aspect in organizations. Organizational cultures are varied and powerful, such that if leaders a) miss this fact or b) do not make a culture work for them, they will take a strategic hit.

My time in government taught me a rich encyclopedia of cultural lessons. I make this point on behalf of government with particular ferocity because of the usual myth that government is all the same. Government culture as a label seems to denote a bureaucratic, faceless, uncaring, and somewhat mediocre atmosphere. That is flat-out ridiculous! Government agencies are comprised of multiple cultures that are particular, deep, fascinating, and a gold mine if leaders appreciate them.

My career in business had built my awareness of the power of organizational culture. Working in everything from a hippy-styled ice cream purveyor to an intensely collaborative virtual consulting firm had taught me that each organization has a unique culture, just as people each have unique personalities. I was, therefore, hardly surprised when I joined government to find multiple cultures and personalities. I am not sure, however, that I could ever have been prepared for its *hundreds* of different subcultures.

GSA's subcultures were fascinating. Some offices were very formal and almost imperious. People fastidiously called me Administrator Johnson, and I felt underdressed if I was not wearing my suit jacket. Other offices at GSA were highly innovative with an open, tumultuous atmosphere reminiscent of companies in Silicon Valley. Staff members played pranks and acquired nicknames. I could take off my suit jacket with them.

The microcultures of government can be heartening to a leader. I was often energized by the variety of ways the human spirit asserted itself in organizational culture. From my position at the top of GSA I was privileged to see and appreciate its many faces. Its variety offered many levers for change. I could spot groups more inclined for certain assignments. Perhaps one was a better place to nurture new talent, while another offered a good setting for a senior, more formal expert. One group could be relied on to handle the first phase of moving into swing space to shake out the wrinkles in the process for the next group. Another might be best for showcasing new security procedures.

The myriad cultures across government add color and interest to the day and present a leader with the opportunity for more thoughtful decision-making. However, those who chafe at the government's monolithic bureaucratic culture are on to something that needs to be described more carefully and understood more completely.

Our governmental organizations have been structured in a way that has created a systemic tension, creating and then pitting the norms of two different cultures against each other. One of these is a culture of rights; the other is a culture of performance.

The result is a festering conflict. All public sector leaders experience it and need to recognize this tension and its root causes so as to attribute its effect more accurately. Leaders will be more successful if they can help us all understand the conflicting constraints placed on them, our shared responsibility for them, and the duality and the trade-offs these constraints compel.

I believe it is this culture war that the public and skeptics sense when they describe government as bureaucratic and sluggish. This conflict presents an ongoing challenge to all public sector leaders.

The Culture of Rights

The roots of the cultural tension reach back to the formation of the civil service. The Pendleton Civil Service Reform Act of 1883 began the delineation of our modern civil service in which government employees are placed in roles based on merit. The political spoils system was cut back dramatically and is allocated with extreme care to this day. Essentially the President only appoints the top executives of any agency, while the rest of the organization is made up of civil service employees.

The resulting rules that protect the civil service are complex and demand lengthy and fastidious due process. Fortified by memories as well as modern incidents of political harassment, the nation has created and reinforced a strong *culture of rights* for workers in government. The rules are on the books to ensure that all government workers are on fair footing in hiring, promotion, and pay.

This creates a strong cultural norm in government. When asked about what I produced as a government worker, part of my answer was that I produced due process. Government is asked to do extraordinary things: defend the borders, issue money, monitor the weather, and so forth. At the same time, it has to be fair to all citizens and respect them. This is institutionalized in a commitment to due process for its own employees as well.

The Culture of Performance

In the latter half of the twentieth century, government was engulfed in another substantial shift. Americans had begun to demand more of industry, insisting on quality products and improved customer service. American industry underwent an extraordinary *performance revolution* in the 1980s and 1990s, and in its wake government also came under pressure for higher performance. Citizens wanted and demanded ever more steadily and loudly that the government produce real, discernable, and consistent value.

In line with this, the government started where it always does, by passing laws. The relatively rapid-fire progression of new legislation was aimed at improving core institutional processes, such as how money was managed, how planning must occur, and how purchasing was done. It sounds rather pedestrian, though not to management geeks. Consider the milestones urging a *gov-*

ernment performance revolution that would ultimately parallel the transformation occurring in industry:

- In 1990, Chief Financial Officers Act pushed federal agencies to manage their money properly by requiring audited financial statements.

- In 1993, Government Performance and Results Act laid out further performance reform.

- In 1994, Government Management Reform Act deepened the 1990 law.

- In 1996, Federal Financial Management Improvement Act augmented previous legislation and required full disclosure of federal financial data.

- Also in 1996, Information Technology Management Reform Act, commonly referred to as the Clinger-Cohen Act, tackled the management of IT, one of the chief tools for management and performance discipline.

Legislation is the starting point in government, as I mentioned earlier. Then it falls to government leaders to integrate the new directions with what is in place.

The new round of rules was meant to be in service of building a *culture of performance*. It sought to legislate performance, just as the earlier laws had sought to legislate a meritocracy. While some argue that the *rights culture* and the *performance culture* are complementary and are pointed in the same direction, the rules and regulations structured for each do not mesh well.

For example, due process (rights culture) requires time. Its primary concern is justice, which involves an elaborate set of rules to explain what is fair, as well as a strict appeal process of complaints, investigations, and even litigation if employees want to elevate concerns. On the other hand, getting results (performance culture) is about immediate and regular response to trends. Transactions, service delivery, and information availability are measured in terms of the time they absorb. Promptness is a virtue that has only been accelerated by new technologies that transmit information instantaneously.

Another angle is that a performance culture expects employees to produce results, focusing on outcomes and outputs. A merit/rights culture, in contrast, expects the process to be exemplary, focusing on inputs, selection, and structures. The potential for rubs and conflict is very real.

Every government leader sits on top of this simmering culture war. On the one hand, civil servants have specific and important protections. On the other, the agencies and departments have been assigned heightened expectations for performance. The two cultures can butt heads.

As leaders seek to drive an agenda for improving service or sharpening programs, they have to be fastidiously certain that they are not encroaching on employees' rights. Consider one scenario. A GSA Public Building Service office encounters a surge of problems: rough weather has caused a flood in a historic courthouse and a collapsed roof in a government laboratory; tenants have been complaining of headaches and odd smells in a downtown office building; construction of yet another complex has been halted due to a shortage of materials. To respond quickly and thoroughly, it would help if more GSA employees could pitch in. Perhaps people from staff offices such as the finance or civil rights groups or from one of the other operating or policy divisions could be reassigned?

Not very easily. Job descriptions and performance agreements might not accommodate those reassignments. Budgets come out of specific categories, and if the money that pays for an employee is restricted, so is the employee's assignment. Formally changing the paperwork or reallocating the proper funds becomes complicated. The option of more generic position descriptions leaves room for misinterpretation and snarled performance reviews and ratings. Flexibility and fairness can find themselves at odds.

It should be noted that a version of this culture tension exists in the business world. Labor unions, worker protection laws, and other structures exist as important avenues to protect employee rights. Flexibility, responsiveness, and speedy performance are simultaneously on the priority list. Tension can occur between the demands for employee rights and business performance. In government, however, there is additional rigidity in the rights culture so as to avoid political influence. Hence the resulting push and pull between the rights and performance cultures has a particular intensity.

My Resignation as a Case Study

My resignation experience offers a case study on the cultural challenges faced by government leaders. The lesson is about the clash between rights and performance culture in an election year, which culminated in political decisions, not strategic organizational decisions.

The Western Regions' Training Conference in Las Vegas was organized and hosted in 2010 by the Pacific Rim Region headquartered in San Francisco. The GSA executive in charge became the focus of the Inspector General's investigation and the IG report raised considerable question about the executive's choices and judgment.

As the scandal unfolded, complete with pictures of the executive in a hot tub, the competing demands of the rights and performance cultures began to assert themselves. The *rights* culture insisted on due process for government employees. The *performance* culture insisted on responsiveness and timely action.

By *rights*, the San Francisco executive deserved an even-handed and deliberate management decision about the consequences for him. He was a career civil servant, entitled to a process that called for a month of reviews and assessments. The time was cordoned off for both his *and* the government's benefit. He would have time to retain counsel, build his case, and review his options. The government, meanwhile, would do its analysis and decision-making.

The *performance* demands on GSA, however, quickly became white hot as the media worked over the story. It was important that I show responsiveness to the concerns that the GSA had made contracting and spending mistakes. The only significant action I could take immediately with respect to the San Francisco executive, however, was to *put him on notice* that he was in trouble and that the clock was now ticking.

The public had no interest in cooler points about GSA's employees' *rights*. Fat chance it would be that a letter of notice to the executive would satiate the news cycle beast and assure the public and Congress that I took the situation seriously. What real options did I have?

For starters, I could launch various internal processes, which I did. I put some people on administrative leave, issued letters of reprimand to others, and set up internal reviews of travel and training events. Obviously these actions did not compare with the kind of dramatic and quick decisions a private sector executive could choose to make. In view of such a point of contrast, in the public eye my responses would appear tepid and sluggish at best.

The people who *could* be immediately disciplined were those serving as the political leadership of the agency and that included me. An appointee serves at the pleasure of the President, who can revoke such offers at will. The merit system and the rights culture apply to political appointees, but in a much more diluted way.

Two appointees at GSA were in the chain of command above the San Francisco executive. Both were friends of mine; one had been a special colleague for over 15 years. They both had more integrity and passion about public service than any other two people I know. Neither had broken contracting rules or squandered money. They simply sat on the organization chart in the boxes above the conference organizers and managers.

As we cycled through the issues and options in meetings at the White House, the political imperative grew. Something dramatic had to be done to counter the damage of the scandal. It was, after all, an election year.

Ultimately, the choice was made to take action with political appointees. On April 2, 2010, I had to fire one of them at 11:30 AM over the phone as he was on vacation with his family. At 1:30 PM I was required to fire the second one in a face-to-face meeting.

I have already told the rest of the story. At 2:00 PM I resigned.

In Conclusion

Public service is an honor and it is a challenge. It is laced with intense constraints, historic context, structural difficulties, harsh politics, and at times very personal risk.

For leaders it offers important lessons about facing tough realities, understanding root causes, applying creativity in the tightest of circumstances, and much more.

CHAPTER FOUR

Leading with Blockbuster Ideas

I spent a couple years working in an architecture business in Boston. As the CFO of a design firm, I watched the numbers while the architects designed hospitals and labs. I was in awe of their ability to juggle multiple dimensions so that from their floor plans windows, plumbing, and safety features landed in the right places. Their designs were also simply beautiful to me. I began to dream of a day when I could live in a house that had been designed to be our home.

Five years later, that is exactly what we were able to do with a small property we bought in Annapolis, Maryland. An architect took our ideas and created a marvelous home. The additional expense of the architect meant we had to forego some details in the construction. Our budget, for example, could not cover built-in bookshelves in the living room, so we delayed that project for later.

After living in the house for a couple of years, we noticed two things. First, we really missed our books, which had been relegated to dozens of boxes in the basement. Second, we were puzzled about how to decorate the dining room. It was a dramatically long rectangle, designed to accommodate *two* tables. I had installed one table for meals and another for all of our family projects (sewing, homework, jigsaw puzzles). Placing furniture along the walls did not look right. China cabinets or sideboards would interrupt the clean, striking length of the room in an unsatisfying way.

One day, staring at the dining room yet again and wondering aloud if painting the walls a different color would help, my husband and I realized something. A dining room is the only room in the house in which all of the furniture is effectively pushed to the center of the room. That was Insight #1.

Conversely, in a living room the furniture is pushed against the walls. That was Insight #2. It took almost no leap to arrive at Insight #3. The dining room walls, therefore, were a much better place for the library shelves. We had a new plan in an instant. We built bookshelves in the dining room.

In short, we had been looking at the dining room and not seeing it as a library.

I love ideas that completely transform a person's thinking. In an instant everything changes. I call such ideas *blockbuster ideas*. They bust up blockheaded notions. They turn the meaning of something on its head. A blockbuster idea can have great impact by redirecting everyone's vision, perception, or cognition.

Blockbuster ideas abound. They can be as mundane as the concept for a dining room or as revolutionary as changing our view of the world from geocentric to heliocentric. We changed everything about math and money with a zero. We took down the tollbooths at one end of tunnels and bridges and doubled the price. The world—or our assumptions about a part of the world—can suddenly and simply change.

As a leader, I look for blockbuster ideas. It is a great thing to find an idea that sparks a metamorphosis in a person's thinking, and it is the same with an organization. When blockbuster ideas are introduced to employees, everyone's thinking is rearranged. The ideas act like large magnets, attracting everyone to them. Fresh approaches and startling new ways of thinking grab attention. Employees are intrigued. The ideas spread as others are also tickled by the new approach. Soon people are energized, galvanized, and paying attention.

Importantly, the magnetic quality pulls everyone in the *same* direction, just as in the wake of a magnet, filings align themselves in an orderly, symmetrical pattern. In organizational terms this alignment is a coveted outcome. When everyone is facing the same direction, the organization is more immediately a team, capable of shared synergy. A common cause can be a powerful thing.

Blockbuster ideas have formed the centerpiece of my tenure in leadership positions. Here are a couple of GSA examples.

Zero Environmental Footprint: Our Pull Metric

Once upon a time, we did not have radar, global positional systems, or other sophisticated navigational technology to steer our way across the high seas. Instead, the captain of a ship relied chiefly on a sextant. He (never a she, I gather) used it to take directional angles from two points: the position of celestial objects and the horizon. Steering a ship was about finding its relationship to the stars and the edge of the world.

To me this is how leaders need to steer their organizations, fixing on points that are part of the large and long view. While it is easy and all too common to get caught up in quarterly earnings and budget cycles, we need to be about steering with vision and targeting a destination point beyond the curve of the earth.

How do we find that point? What sextant can leaders use in our modern world?

Early in my career I was part of a transformation anchored in a single and simple metric. Our goal at Cummins Engine Company was to produce a perfect diesel engine, one of absolute unassailable quality, or to be specific, with no defects. There was a lot of philosophy and technique attached to this program, but the core direction, the magnet that pulled us all, was the goal of a perfect product, produced again and again ... without flaw.

I call that magnet a *pull metric*. It created a force, a pull for change, by describing a single point on the horizon. Everyone grasped its merit and importance. People cared about it and joined in the effort. Employees stood tall because they were engaged in the effort of producing something extraordinary, repeatedly. Taking each step with the same goal in mind, we figured out how to head toward that point on the horizon together. The work produced results, built an organizational reputation, and spawned an upward spiral of excellence. It also pulled all of the activity of the organization in a specific direction.

As the commonly appreciated and priority value, it had the power to affect the thousands of decisions, processes, routines, and adjustments that occur each day in an organization. People were willing and energized to review and adjust each element in the mix so that it would support the pull metric. If it did not, it was ignored or discarded. In effect, each activity was performed against the reference point of the pull metric. Our activity was *reverse-engineered* from it.

Specifically, at the Cummins Jamestown Engine Plant in upstate New York, we had to learn not to feed the iconic American assembly line from the front end, line-setting blocks and hoping for the best. It meant moving beyond the chaos that is parodied in the *I Love Lucy* episode in the chocolate factory. She could not sort and pack fast enough, and soon she was stuffing candy in her pockets and mouth to keep them from cascading off the belt.

We had to solve problems for good instead of kicking them down the assembly line. The "pull" of the customer expecting a perfect engine drove us. We had to throw away old crutches, such as the expensive dependence on racks and racks of inventory for any eventuality. We could not expect engines to make it through production and out the door without assuring that pacing, tools, training, and parts were absolutely synchronized.

Suppliers formally agreed to an uninterrupted flow of quality parts. Engineers reconfigured the assembly line so that parts arrived closer to the assembly workers and in smaller quantities. A team of metal workers set up a workshop to fabricate all kinds of tools, gimmicks, and equipment that would help assembly teams do their jobs with fewer steps and less movement. And more. Much more. The culture and discipline that formed have been further honed and nurtured in that Cummins plant to this day.

The pull metric revolution has been happening across American business for more than four decades. It has inspired a reinvention of processes, rework of the supply chain, re-education and reinvigoration of the workforce, and a shift in the role of leadership. The result has been a *performance revolution* across America. It has also been transferred as a management concept into government, education and other arenas.

Examples of Other Pull Metrics

I have been collecting examples of pull metrics for some time. All of them have DNA that goes back to the ancestral pull metric, Total Quality Management (TQM) introduced to the United States by W. Edwards Deming. He first helped Japan reboot its industrial base in the 1950s.

Japan eventually demonstrated its new ability to produce products repeatedly at high levels of quality and transformed its reputation on the international economic stage. Its dramatic improvement and performance became a huge gauntlet thrown down to challenge American industry.

Many organizations jumped on the Total Quality bandwagon. Soon, though, other American enterprises adopted pull metrics that were better fitted to their own needs and circumstances.

Alcoa, for example, chose to focus on perfect safety. In some industries such as mining or metal processing where work could be quite dangerous, employees were deeply concerned about safety. Like poor quality, a poor safety record will cost an organization a great deal in resources, time, and reputation. Total safety became another huge magnet for transformation. Organizations would reverse-engineer all of their processes to guarantee that excruciating carefulness was routine. Such attention to detail improved products as well as safety.

Service industries have evolved their own versions of the pull metric. The hotel industry has reinvented processes as well as empowered employees to make decisions on the spot to assure the absolute best customer service.

The Ritz Carlton, for example, adopted as its pull metric a demanding *exquisite service* standard: "we are ladies and gentlemen serving ladies and gentlemen." The Ritz aimed for a "Wow!" from both customers and staff. To get there they changed systems, processes, training, selection, and more.

Enterprise Cars has done an exceptional job of placing its customers truly in the driver's seat by reverse-engineering its services from that single point and relying on a measure of how much the customer promotes Enterprise to others.

Fewer examples of the pull metric exist in government. While the Total Quality phrase has been embedded in the language of many federal bureaucracies, it has not been used as a powerful transformational tool for changing the entire organization. That is not to say that it cannot happen. Its promise, however, has not been exploited.

Nevertheless, I have been inspired by the snippet of a story I heard from a consultant over a decade ago. It illuminates how a government organization could think in pull metric terms and realize a great deal of improvement as a result. The story was about the Human Resources department within one of the military services when the nation was engaged in the Gulf War. The detail around the story made me think it was a bit of an urban myth, but it makes my point.

The Human Resources group in the story wanted to change to become more effective. They decided to focus on a surprising pull metric: to aim for a perfect *bereavement call.* This is, of course, the call paid to a family to inform them of the death of a loved one. Difficult and tragic as that duty is, the goal was perfection: no bureaucracy, accurate scheduling, completely clear and sympathetic communications, accurate information, and timely staffing assignments. Viewed through the lens of a pull metric, anyone can see how employees would be motivated by this goal. To achieve it, they would easily support the reverse engineering of processes and become engaged in wringing mistakes out of their system.

I Wanted a Pull Metric at GSA

When I was sworn in at GSA, I knew I wanted a pull metric for GSA, to support the transformation it needed, and additionally position it to help the government transform. I knew the *deep and lasting* power of the pull metric from my experience at Cummins.

It had been extraordinary to see a system completely transform itself under extreme competitive pressure and with a deeply inspiring vision. It gave me absolute and complete confidence that massive, resource-intensive, highly skilled organizations can turn on a dime with the right leadership and ideas.

I also knew that the pull metric was a godsend because it deals with the vision thing. Organizations do better when employees have a shared vision. It helps if they are aiming for the same point on the horizon.

It is not easy to agree on or crystallize the vision, however. I have sat through too many visioning sessions in organizations not to know that they can wallow in two things: the endless activity of wordsmithing and a conversation that is heartfelt and aspirational but does not connect to useful plans and action. The pull metric is a terrific bridge between the jargon stratosphere and the day-to-day world. It creates a direct line from vision to employee engagement, better performance, improved processes, efficiency and effectiveness, improved partnerships with customers and suppliers, and more. What's not to like?

No one could be surprised that, with this as my history and experience, I started looking for a pull metric the minute I walked in the door at GSA, but the answer was not immediately obvious. Government is a messy business. GSA was not a linear production line. It was more like a laundry list of activities. How could a pull metric work in such a crosshatched, widespread, apples-and-oranges enterprise?

Furthermore, what particular pull metric would work? Total quality had in some respects run its course. Plenty of people understood its power, but engaging in a total quality metric effort would mean remembering and revisiting GSA's TQM process that had petered out in the 1990s.

Did perfect safety make any sense? Not much of what we did had the edge of hazard to it. Perhaps in parts of our construction work it might make sense, but safety was not a priority in an organization full of contracting officers.

In the wake of September 11, the government had obsessed about security. Would there be any benefit or value in naming complete security as our pull metric? If we linked it to cyber security, there could be some interesting possibilities for parts of GSA. However, perfect security would not be a pull metric that would inherently engage all people across the organization.

Much of GSA's work involved providing services. Should we shoulder a pull metric that embraced our customers in the manner of Enterprise Rent-A-Car? Some of our services were practically at the retail level. Our building managers were in constant communication with tenants in response to their needs and questions. But many of our services were so embedded in large contracts (financial services, for example) that the notion of exquisite service became lost in the legal language of the deal. Moreover, it was contractors, not GSA staff, who were in customers' immediate line of sight.

None of the pull metrics used successfully by others galvanized us. When we considered them for GSA, they were pedestrian ideas, not blockbusters. Fortunately, within weeks of my arrival, our pull metric simply fell into my lap. This is how it happened.

I entered the Administrator's job as the American Recovery and Reinvestment Act of 2009 was unfolding. GSA was already hard at work channeling funds to enhance building performance by installing photovoltaic panels, changing out inefficient windows, replacing lights, mounting better sensors, programming computers to adjust temperatures, and assessing energy usage in buildings.

One intention of this effort was to help support the flailing construction industry. However, another intention was to stimulate job growth, particularly in new green businesses where innovative ideas were being turned into reality. An environmental focus meant innovation.

There were other green activities elsewhere in the organization. We were improving the fleet's efficiency, creating policies to encourage more environmental choices in purchasing, assessing the energy impact of our own data centers, and more. In these cases, an environmental focus meant efficiencies and costs savings.

Green was a twofer. If GSA worked on environmental and energy projects, we could help the economy by stimulating innovation and creating jobs. We could also reduce waste: wasted energy, wasted fuel, and wasted resources. Green was about innovation *and* no waste.

It worked. The pull metric could be about environmental impact. Every corner of GSA was either about efficiency (reducing waste/cost) and/or about innovation (helping the government into the future). All we needed to do was to bake this into a single unifying metric.

What environmental metric was right? I briefly entertained a discussion of the kinds of numbers and dates that would be stretch goals. How about reducing our environmental footprint by 40 percent by 2025, for example? Each goal formulation was challenging, but ultimately random.

What sealed my thinking was reminding myself that a pull metric is not a stretch goal. It is the horizon and stars. It is the farthest you can go. It defies possibility in its most extreme. It is about perfection. In our case it had to be zero. The logic unfolded rapidly. GSA would adopt, absolutely and audaciously, a pull metric of Zero Environmental Footprint. We immediately shortened it to ZEF.

Interface Gave GSA a Model

ZEF caught on quickly at GSA.

Why? The agency had a deep history of energy conservation. It built the first federal green roof in the 1970s. The energy efficiency in GSA buildings was significantly better than private sector counterparts (over 20 percent) because of early government investment in design and construction. In addition, GSA had been working hard on the efficiency of its vehicle fleet through data and maintenance monitoring. It also had a significant innovation legacy reaching back to and including the lease for an EV1, the electric car that General Motors produced in the 1990s.

In the late 1990s GSA had hosted Ray Anderson, CEO of Interface, a carpet design and manufacturing company in Georgia. He spoke about committing his company to *Mission Zero by 2020,* an extreme environmental goal that meant driving their net energy consumption to nothing by the year 2020.

Reducing their environmental footprint all the way to zero was upending them in good and fascinating ways. He told stories of how they were reinventing their entire business, including product design, supply chain, manufacturing process, training, financial structures, and more.

In 2010, I decided GSA leadership should take another look at the Interface story. First, we learned what it meant for the Interface folks to re-imagine and reinvent their *entire* business. For example, their waste stream had to become their supply stream. They needed used carpet to recycle and feed into the maw of their carpet production process, where fibers and other materials would be reclaimed and reused. To find enough used carpets, they had to scour the country and develop new sources. They went so far as to park trucks at college campuses in order to haul away old carpets after the dorms emptied out in the summer.

Interface also explored different sales models. They began to favor the idea of leasing their carpets, instead of only selling them. Leasing allowed Interface to retain ownership and eased the work of finding and reclaiming old carpet.

The company reworked its product design as well. They adopted and perfected the idea of carpet squares, the stiff tiles of carpet that are now ubiquitous as floor covering in large public spaces. Carpet squares reduced the need to replace entire rooms of carpet when only a section had become faded or worn.

They nursed every inch of their manufacturing process, even coaxing out better ways of sewing together massive rolls of carpet so that the last few inches would not require trimming and become waste. Pallets, spindles, and bobbins were recycled.

None of the details of their story was lost on the GSA team. Each person from a different functional area seemed to see something that was particularly relevant to his or her area of responsibility. Mission Zero at Interface had offered a motivation to review and improve seemingly every corner of the GSA enterprise. We were impressed by the comprehensiveness of the change that was occurring there and what it promised for us.

Second, we learned that Mission Zero was not a program. It was not the whim of the Interface leadership or the flavor-of-the-month. The vision and concepts were woven into every aspect of the organization's activity and behavior. It meant change at every level, engaging the entire workforce, and thus assuring itself a long legacy.

Finally, and critically, we learned how sustainability was dependent on constant new design and innovation. It was not enough to squeeze waste out of the system. Leaders and employees alike had to explore different approaches, always leaning into the future.

For example, Interface has worked to dematerialize their products, reducing or finding alternatives to using resources that require extraction, processing, and shipping. They have worked to abandon glue and find other adhesive and attachment systems for carpet squares. They have employed "bio-mimicry" to find new answers in nature's systems.

If there was anything that truly convinced me about our Zero Environmental Footprint pull metric, it was that third insight. Interface's Mission Zero was about cutting, shrinking, squeezing, trimming *and* innovating. That was the example I wanted GSA to emulate.

The entire GSA leadership team recognized the blockbuster potential of the idea. They readily agreed to support setting our sights on Zero Environmental Footprint, ZEF. If Interface could do it, so could we. And if GSA could do it, so could the entire government. In fact, if the government was to reach a better level of environmental performance, GSA had to be in the game.

It's hard to describe a leader's joy when an organization makes such a major collective strategic decision. GSA's executives were ready to change the world by changing their own processes and performance.

They were a team despite their various business lines. They understood that they were positioned strategically to have impact across the entire government. Each person was quick to grasp that ZEF was a leadership ticket. The shared vision and direction gave them power, the power of a clear and salient idea. They knew the organization would fall in line enthusiastically. Best of all, they had a concrete pull metric, a tool for moving forward. We were not waving wands and wishing hard. We were collectively inspired and getting down to work.

Putting ZEF to Work

Adopting a blockbuster idea is a significant turning point for an organization. A good bit of the past comes under scrutiny. The future, however, is not entirely clear. We had agreed to a major pull metric effort, yet at the outset we did not really know its entire scope. We couldn't have. We did not know what we did not know. This made planning a little tricky.

Once we declared ZEF to be our goal, GSA went to work. In government terms, that meant we started planning, analyzing, studying, and generally getting acquainted with a new direction. We also began to get into action.

We studied and adopted policies that could be changed to favor more green process and expenditures in government. We looked at the industry to see what was happening in the next phases of energy information and efficiency in buildings, and we began to volunteer our buildings as test beds. We explored how to take our fleet and travel programs to an even more efficient level.

We championed the new telework legislation, which encouraged government employees to work in various places outside the office and took its direction to create our own teleworking policies and activities. This led logically to approaches to reduce commuting and tackle the proliferation of space under lease and rent across government.

We pointed out the obvious truism: if you want to reduce the environmental footprint of buildings, the biggest bang comes from reducing the actual physical footprint. This set us up for *another* blockbuster idea, the workplace of the future, which I describe later in the next section.

As our momentum built, we discovered much that we didn't know or hadn't seriously considered. One surprise was electronic waste, often referred to as e-waste. Some knew of this issue, but it had not yet grown into a widely understood issue of public concern. Not many of us even understood the dimensions of the e-waste problem. Among other things, it pollutes the ground, endangers workers who handle it casually, and drains stocks of limited and precious materials.

It turned out that e-waste was a staggeringly big story. Government's role in the issue was huge. We did some calculations in regard to computers only (not phones, hand-held devices, televisions, video cameras, and so on) and were stunned at the picture that appeared: **the government disposes of roughly 10,000 computers a week!**

It works out like this:

- Take 2,000,000 federal employees

- Multiply by an 80 percent estimate of how many employees have computers = 1,600,000 computers

- Multiply by 33 percent, because computers are replaced approximately every three years = 528,000 old computers being replaced annually

- Divide by 52 weeks in a year = 10,153 old computers being cast off every week.

Let's repeat: *the government disposes roughly 10,000 computers a week!*

What happens to all of those computers? What *should* happen to all those computers? They certainly should not go into landfills. Does anyone use them? What do *they* do with them?

GSA started to address e-waste by partnering with other agencies. As the government's agent for property disposal, GSA had a part to play, but the entire government was involved. Other agencies understood the environmental issues and the international trade concerns, since electronic waste is bought and shipped (and dumped) across national borders.

Relatively quickly, we were able to issue guidelines for government e-waste disposal, thus raising awareness, diverting a significant waste stream away from landfills and toward certified recyclers, and demonstrating our commitment.

Taking on the issue of electronic waste demonstrates the tremendous value of a pull metric. Its methodology requires a reverse-engineering perspective that digs back and into systems. In the process, things can be eliminated, smoothed, and changed. In addition, the process can uncover critical systems that need attention. In this and other ways Zero Environmental Footprint started to pull us through changes and into an innovative, more responsible, and more efficient future.

ZEF is a pull metric, and pull metrics constitute a blockbuster idea. Pull metrics can stimulate a deep shift in process and culture. That is the kind of change that has staying power. The leader who presides over such a shift builds legacy, although not a legacy that is flashy or showy. This kind of legacy is about deep systemic improvement in the nature of the organization and its capabilities.

Government leaders struggle with legacy. With changes in administration, a leader's work can be disrupted, abandoned, and forgotten. It is very difficult to maintain momentum for change. When process and culture are affected, however, deep change and stickiness result. The workforce benefits. Employees are not likely to erase methods that save them time, prevent mistakes, and stop do-overs. Pull metrics, therefore, introduce an organization to a method for innovation, systemic change, and permanent improvement.

The Workplace of the Future

I joined GSA at a sweet spot in time. Change was in the air for organizations. With dramatic shifts in mobile technologies and communications devices as well as globalization, industry was in constant transformation. Enterprises were less dependent on geographic proximity and more interested in supporting networks and collaboration.

As a result, work was being redefined, and workspace was being redesigned.

Government had not yet fallen in line. In fact, I was not so sure it had even gotten the message! Yes, a few political leaders, mostly at the local levels, were urging more collaboration. Mayor Adrian Fenty in Washington, D.C., and Mayor Michael Bloomberg in New York City had made a point of working in open offices, surrounded by staff, emulating the newsrooms we have all seen in the movies.

There was little such innovation in the federal system. The military had its ongoing wrestling match among the services to find ways of managing jointly. The intelligence community was largely out of sight, but we all knew about its difficulties in working together seamlessly. For the most part, federal government exemplified the old values of hierarchy, stovepipes, and careful protection of territory. Only in special cases were task forces created or interdisciplinary issues worked successfully. Collaboration was not the norm.

GSA, by dint of its mandate and size, had a big opportunity to help bring government along on this revolution. Responsible for workspace, for helping government be more effective, and for spotting the capabilities that new technologies offered, GSA could be a major strategic force in effecting *new ways for government to work*. The case for change was building. The problems were more and more obvious. The time was right.

Let's back up to paint some specifics of the scene.

Space Needs Are Shifting and Rent Bills Are High

The federal government's footprint is pretty darned big. GSA manages over 360 million square feet of space. If your house is 2,000 square feet, the GSA portfolio would be equivalent to 175,000 homes the size of yours. As you can imagine, the government pays a lot in rent for all that workspace. While salaries are the largest single administrative charge to an agency's budget, rent is usually the second in amount.

Surprisingly, federal office buildings, like many office buildings in the private sector, are quite empty. Agencies traditionally obtain, rent, or lease buildings so each employee can have a workspace, whether an office, cubicle, or lab station. The space is, of course, heated or cooled, furnished, secured, and wired. But the turnstiles in the lobbies of various buildings that track people entering and leaving almost always tell us that a given building is on average underutilized. It is not used steadily or efficiently.

For example, on Tuesday, Wednesday, and Thursday, it is common for only 40 to 50 percent of employees to come into an office building. On Monday and Friday the number is even lower—below 40 percent—and dipping at times into the 20 percent range.

Where is everyone? They are attending to business, but not in their offices. They could be at conferences, external meetings, depositions, or hearings. Many are patrolling in cars, inspecting sites, or investigating cases. Others are with clients or program recipients, in training, or on travel coordinating with other branches of the organization. Furthermore, employees are entitled to a certain amount of personal time spent away from the office.

Take note that the federal government is mostly a first shift (or day shift) enterprise. This means that its office space is not only underutilized during first shift hours, but it is completely empty during both second and third shift hours. No one is surprised that it is also entirely vacant on weekends. Therefore, the government is paying for real estate that may be fully occupied (meaning that it is fully assigned to real people), but is nevertheless unused more than 80 percent of the week.

I am arguing the general case, not the specific one. Various organizations have needs that change this equation: they run prisons, handle intelligence, manage hospitals, sail ships, or work in secure labs. These require space not just dedicated to employees, but space also dedicated to function. Such space is often open for business around the clock with full attendant staff.

For a good many federal workers, though, the government maintains fulltime space for much less than fulltime need. This is hardly a problem unique to government. The private sector faces the same dilemma.

Flexibility Is Increasing

Technology has dramatically changed how many of us are able to work. Of course, if you are running a day care center, you need to be at work, physically present for the children. However, many people engage in work that is portable.

Employees can now work seamlessly in any number of locations—home, library, airport—because they are supported by smart phones, laptops, shared files, and various applications. The private sector has embraced a lot of this capability. Workers everywhere are adjusting to the new options. Coffee shops are the new conference rooms. Universities offer courses online. Despite telework legislation, progress in government was exceedingly cautious and slow.

Getting to Work Is Tougher

Commuting has become more demanding, expensive, and energy-consuming. Long drives cost people in time, money, peace of mind, and stiff muscles. Transportation systems are not keeping up. Employees are robbed of family time, community time, down time, and much more, when they are stuck on the roads in traffic.

Collaboration Is More Crucial

The nature of work, even in government, is shifting. Public servants used to perform their jobs in a fairly severe hierarchy. The chain of command still dominates, but the problems and issues are more and more cross-functional. Government workers need to reach across the organizational charts, to gather and share information broadly. Sitting in the boss' line of sight is not of much value. Employees need to be out and about, or hooked in from anywhere to online affinity groups. It is a different and absolutely essential approach to work these days.

Productivity Is about Smart Measurement, Not Control

In the old days, a boss watched workers to see that they were doing their work. One GSA employee told me a story of her early days in the government when the boss had on his desk a bell that he would ring periodically. All staff would put down their pencils so that he could check that the right work was being done. Sounds like junior high!

We are much smarter today about measuring outcomes, tracking usage, and staying in touch through social media. Seeing employees is no longer always about physical proximity. It can be done by checking if their chat lines are open, tracking computer key strokes, or using video, as well as by agreeing explicitly as a workgroup to check in from the road and file materials by deadlines.

GSA Has a Reputation for Innovative Real Estate Management

I was both mildly surprised and gratified when I visited the Google headquarters in California. After a good discussion about information technology and innovation, we were scheduled to have lunch with Google's facilities staff. I was not entirely sure I had read the schedule correctly. Why visit Google to talk about real estate?

It turned out that their facilities staff had requested the meeting because they were bowled over by GSA's real estate management performance. They wanted to hear more about our sustainability work and Design Excellence program, and pick our brains about managing such a vast inventory.

I was reminded repeatedly while in office that GSA is a tremendous model and driver for many corners of industry, including real estate. GSA has vast influence both because of size and because of innovation and expertise, including energy efficiency, historical preservation, support of the arts, and more. If the workplace is changing, GSA belongs in the thick of it.

Finding Synergy in a Blockbuster Idea about the Workplace

Given all of the above contextual pressures and GSA's posture for innovation, a blockbuster idea emerged: the Workplace of the Future. The concept stitched together all of the trends and pointed GSA in a single direction.

If people cannot get to work easily and technology can support them elsewhere, why not help that happen? If buildings are a big expense but not much in use, why not redesign them to be more efficient? Most revolutionary, if work is flexible, why not treat space as flexible?

As with ZEF, this blockbuster idea was built out of partnership across the agency. GSA's Public Buildings Service was particularly committed to building and managing workspace creatively. The Federal Acquisition Service was engaged in provisioning government workers so that their technology allowed flexibility and new work styles. GSA's policy office promoted new ways to do government work.

Importantly, this blockbuster idea was not about inventing new ways of working, but about showcasing and modeling what was already occurring in industry and schools. Bringing it into government was a game changer. GSA needed to help government work better. Concentrating on *how and where* it worked could turn the government's face to the future.

Quickly, the plans and activities took shape. The idea was powerful. GSA was eager to build interest and capability by seeding examples, running prototypes, and building infrastructure. The agency started to focus on the following:

- *Reconfigured Workspace*: GSA's real estate, furniture, policy, and technology people shifted their support for tenants by encouraging more flexible work environments. Customers chose from the full menu of GSA expertise in order to design space, redesign work, adjust HR policies, reconfigure technology, and understand metrics.

- *Data Analysis:* The Public Building Service put together projects to gather data about building utilization so that tenants could see good business arguments for changing their approach to workspace.

- *Information Access:* Shaking off the mystery of putting information in the cloud was necessary to encourage the government as a whole to view it as a viable option. Employees needed to access their files and information from wherever they were working. The cloud would help. Within weeks of starting my job, I was plotting with

GSA's Chief Information Officer on how to move us into the cloud quickly so we could make the point.

- *Workspace Assignment Logistics:* If employees did not have assigned offices, they needed a place to tag workspaces for the hours they were in the building. GSA implemented scheduling software that mapped the workspaces and allowed workers to sign into a workspace efficiently for time slots ranging from an hour to a week or more.

- *Workplace Flexibility:* GSA championed telework. Agency staff developed metrics for teams to use to confirm and assess the work they did in places other than the office. GSA joined the government-wide Telework Week annually, taking advantage of the fanfare to insist our own employees give it a try. Various managers started to telework. Some closed their offices and worked out of briefcases, backpacks, and very large purses for a month. They recorded their experiences on video and analyzed the lessons they learned.

The more GSA shouldered the blockbuster idea of the Workplace of the Future, the more everyone learned, and the agency expanded its expertise and support. In the midst of this work, a once-in-a-century opportunity emerged to showcase the Workplace of the Future.

The GSA headquarters building in Washington, D.C., was the last of the major historic legacy government headquarters to be renovated. Built in 1917, the building at 1800 F Street had received very little attention and had grown quite long in the tooth. Its hallways were shabby and dark, the infrastructure was terribly out of date, vast ropes of cables looped along the ceilings, doors were broken, and air conditioners hung out of every window. It was unsightly and drab. Luckily, the American Recovery and Reinvestment Act of 2009 provided funds to start renovations.

I remember the decisive meeting with Robert Peck, the Commissioner of the Public Buildings Service, when we reviewed budgets and schedules for the headquarters renovations and agreed on a dramatically new direction.

"How far can we go?" I asked.

"We have a big chance here. It's a distinctive and historic building near the White House, and it has the size and location to make a major statement," Bob mused. "And, since we've used the current configuration for a century, we have to design the new configuration to hold up through the next century."

"I can't read the future. I don't know what office buildings will be like in 2110. No one has a crystal ball that good," I responded.

"Then, let's build it for as many contingencies as possible, for the most flexibility. We can open it up, use natural light, and treat it like a shell for activity, rather than a map of activity."

"And let's make it for all GSA so we can finally have a cohesive headquarters. Can we move everyone in?"

Bob paused for barely a split second. "From the other leased buildings? I don't see why not. We'll run the numbers so we have clear analysis to support it. If we treat the building as open and flexible, rather than as reserved space, many more people can call it their base of operations. If we consolidate everyone into it, there could be significant cost savings to boot."

The deal was done. We were not renovating a government headquarters to suit what we could predict out 10 or 15 years. We were committing to a vision of the next century in which space, technology, footprint, flexibility, and work styles were going to change and change again. We simply could not recreate workspace for the present norms. We could not let the government be satisfied with that.

We never looked back.

Bob did not wait for the renovations to begin. He promptly reconfigured his own office. The large corner Commissioner's office soon housed five people at tables arranged in a cluster in the middle of the room. Bob sat at one end with his deputy next to him and his chief of staff on the other side, and two others filled out the cluster. The offices those people vacated became conference rooms and shared space. Bob claimed an immediate boost in efficiency, since he no longer had to walk up and down the hallways finding people. His gesture showcased how easy it was to free up space for additional people and collaborative work.

When renovations began in late 2010, a large number of employees moved out of the historic headquarters building into temporary swing space. There we started to practice new work-place concepts even more energetically.

For example, we noticed how much was trashed as people cleaned out their old offices. People can become hoarders when they stay in one place too long. With more and more work done online and people moving around more often, and therefore purging their paperwork regularly, space for files could be dra-matically reduced. Hoarding was eliminated. We cut the number of file cabinets in swing space, only to learn over time that we could probably have cut it again by half.

In another instance, we learned about noise management. People started using earbuds and headphones routinely to block the sounds of other people talking. The building was outfitted with white noise to screen or blur some sounds. Small rooms were designated for long phone calls or private conversations. If people found noise a problem, there were options, including working somewhere else for a time, for handling it. In short, as we worked in the building, we found more answers than we had previously imagined.

Another fundamental issue became more sharply defined: what is the meaning and use of space? GSA began to wrestle with the differences among personal space, private space, reserved space, and permanently assigned space. Should some people have space that was permanently assigned to them? Why? How would that be determined? What was fair? Yes, the day care center should be an assigned space, secured and walled off. What about employee counselors? What about the external financial auditors who need files kept under lock and key? The agency became more nuanced about the variety of demands on a building.

The possibility of working in a very different physical environment also surfaced valuable questions about the *workforce* and what it needs to do its best work. For example, it became apparent that younger workers want flexibility but are not keen on fulltime telework, since they want to spend time with mentors, meet people, and build work relationships and networks. Their social needs were perhaps stronger than those of a longer-term employee.

We identified and clarified the sheer mechanics of working in an open building where offices are largely unassigned. An online reservations system was set up to help employees book workstations or conference rooms for the times they will be in the building. Some "touchdown" workstations are reserved for very short use (up to two hours) allowing people to work between meetings but not claim a desk for an entire day when it is not needed. There are explicit team protocols, workspace sharing agreements, copier courtesies, such as stocking empty paper drawers, and the like.

Blockbuster ideas help move organizations to new places and transform even basic assumptions about work and services. GSA was no different. Everywhere we pushed at the notion of the Workplace of the Future, we were challenged to do better.

I was still at GSA when the old interior walls were torn down at 1800 F Street. It was delightful to see the light stream in, flooding newly opened spaces. It was already clear to me that by opening up and changing the workspace in our own headquarters, we were opening up our own understanding of how we ourselves did work. Thus we became genuinely and personally experienced in the changes that we could support for our government customers.

As this book goes to press, GSA has moved back into the renovated headquarters. The blockbuster idea of the Workplace of the Future has become a reality.

GSA's, and eventually the government's, approach to doing its work is, of necessity, evolving. Better collaboration, greater flexibility, and relevant innovation will be important to government institutions' success in addressing the evolving needs of the nation. Nothing can become a new norm until someone starts the work. GSA's blockbuster idea to instigate the Workplace of the Future provided such a spark toward improving government relevance and effectiveness.

Grand SLAMs

Blockbuster ideas are not always of the stuff that gets headlines. One of my favorite blockbuster ideas was a quieter effort to accelerate problem solving. We called them SLAMs. Let me set the stage for why SLAMs are brilliant. Then I will describe how they work.

There Is Never Enough Time ...

As I mentioned in an earlier chapter, it took me almost a year to be sworn into my job as the Administrator at GSA. Even the President remarked publicly on the frustration that the situation evoked. While waiting and waiting for the Senate to vote on my confirmation, I often thought of chronic complaints about the long time it takes to get a government job. The same is often true outside government. When I worked for an executive search firm, I regularly counseled people that changing jobs takes nine months, at a minimum.

By the time I was finally sworn into office, I had lost over 25 percent of the time available during President Obama's first term. Of course, I could not know that my already shortened tenure would be further curtailed by the scandal over the Western Regions' Training Conference in Las Vegas. The fact was that the window of time I had in office was very short.

Waiting had certainly been hard, but there was little else I could do. And then, WHAM! My first day at GSA arrived. It was like a rocket launch, as I walked through the magnetometers at the front door. I vaguely remember greeting staff, setting up my computer passwords, reviewing the schedule, and unpacking personal items at my desk.

After a few hours of "administrivia," however, my time turned into a whirl that did not stop the entire time I was in office. It reminded me of my feelings when the contractions started, and my husband tore up the streets driving me to the hospital. There is no stopping. This baby is yours.

Like people who work on the floor of the stock exchange, in air traffic control towers, or in hospital emergency rooms, I like the thrill of keeping a fast pace. GSA, however, left me gasping. My Chief of Staff would brief me in the elevator between meetings. The email tsunami never stopped, and I would forget to drink my coffee ... when I had time to get some. I found myself talking fast and faster. The cartoon character, Roadrunner, has everything on leaders because he gets to stop between his mad dashes; leaders rarely catch a real break.

Truth be told, however, it is not unusual to have a short window and a busy schedule. Ask an entrepreneur opening a restaurant or a parent who works full time. Frenzy is a day-to-day reality for many of us.

... And Problems Are Daunting

What is unusual is how fast a leader needs to move because of the *consequence* of the position. Problems faced by leaders of large organizations are massive, complicated, and important. A great deal can be lost as time slips by on them. Each day is hugely significant. When I stepped through the door at GSA, the clock was ticking, and there were gigantic tasks to accomplish:

> *Energy Costs*: It is downright hard to manage the heating and cooling of huge office buildings. Think about it this way: every day hundreds of little heaters (people

with a body temperature of 98.6 Fahrenheit) walk in, around, and out of a building.

The problem of tracking and adjusting to the dynamic movement of a building's population is an example of the many moving parts a building manager must address to find energy efficiencies. Energy management also includes installing monitors, finding money to invest in technology, learning about and assessing energy management innovations, negotiating with landlords to upgrade equipment, changing tenant behavior, and more.

For GSA, this work was paramount for thousands of buildings across the nation. It is specifically complex in each building because of variations in location, construction, age, and more. When overall costs are tabulated, there is significant consequence.

- *Excessive Leasing Portfolio*: Too many federal agencies pay for workspace that is leased. It is an expensive option both in the short term and the long term. Leasing allows for flexibility, such as when the Census Bureau needs office space for a few months every ten years. In that situation, the additional cost can be justified against the cost of owning and maintaining a building for the interim nine years.

  Flexibility, however, is not a priority for a courthouse, for instance. Citizens expect that justice will be dispensed for decades, if not centuries, to come.

  Nevertheless, *well over half* of the 360 million square feet of space in GSA's portfolio is leased. That amounts to over 8100 leased properties, which, in March of 2013, was reported to cost the government an annual amount in rent of $5,573,164,929.

  At the heart of the problem is the government's peculiar approach to money. Ongoing expenses are funded by the annual federal budget, which is supported by debt, while capital projects such as constructing courthouses require money in the bank ahead of time.

This has always struck me as completely backward, but it is the consequence of specific budget rules and, of course, politics. As a result of these rules, GSA cannot easily finance the construction or renovation of workspace. The Public Building Fund was established in part to build up a piggy bank for construction, but it is funded parsimoniously, so that ultimately, government tenants end up in more expensive leased space.

- *Skilled Workers*: Contract officers are in very short supply in government. They are rare because they are uniquely skilled in an impressive panoply of expertise in law, business, finance, accounting, acquisition regulations, contract negotiations, and human psychology. The private sector aggressively recruits people with government contracting knowledge, because they are valuable in building strategies for winning government bids. Retirements have drawn down the number of contracting officers, and the sheer stress of the job takes its toll. Even Congress worries about the shortage.

  How can this intensely specialized and undervalued workforce be replenished quickly, and at minimal expense? GSA has its own need of sharp contracting officers and can only do its job well if other agencies have equally proficient employees. Talent management is a challenge that affects everyone in government. (This problem was to haunt me, too, because contracting decisions and mistakes were at the heart of GSA's Las Vegas training conference scandal.)

Leaders want to solve such sticky problems. I sure did. What a contribution it would be to clear them off the decks! What a legacy!

Problem Solving Is a Rough Process

The problem is that often these are *wicked problems*. Not only is there no one answer but, instead, they require large communities to negotiate solutions collectively. To get to a solution demands, at the very least, a three-point run around the bases.

Point one is about getting people on board. Each serious problem calls first for enlisting the community involved, namely, all of the stakeholders who touch the problem or have pieces of the solution. Herding those people together is inordinately difficult.

I used to wake up in the morning with a great solution for some problem. I would mull it over during breakfast. Once in the car, I would mentally start a roster of those who needed to hear the idea. By the time I reached Highway 50, the list would be sizeable and still growing. When I reached the District of Columbia line, I would be worrying about how to get everyone together. Pulling into the parking garage, I would think of the day's work, and my excitement over my idea would start to fade. When would I find time to corral everyone together to work the issue? By the time I got to the elevators, the idea was gone.

The second point focuses on unearthing options. This requires analyzing the problem and arraying the best options for a solution. Finding the experts, tapping into their knowledge, and brainstorming can be tough. People are scattered and busy. They offer their ideas when they get to it.

Point three is about making decisions. Choosing among options requires decisiveness in the face of tough trade-offs. The process can erode as people poke, prod, or play politics. Tick tock ....

At times I nearly threw in the towel. People, options, and decisions were each a painful stage in a cycle that would only plod along. It was enough to make me want to jump out of my skin. Skipping steps or taking shortcuts only forces the process to back up and repeat itself from the beginning. How to find a solution *fast, or at minimum, faster?*

Compressed Problem Solving Events

Goaded by these frustrations during my first months at GSA, I introduced the *SLAM*, a blockbuster idea for accelerating the journey to solutions.

The concept was not original to me. I was familiar with significant literature and many examples of creating an arena for a mass solution. AmericaSpeaks, for example, is an organization that creates large-scale town meeting events to bring all stakeholders together around problems. General Electric is famous for its own version, which they call a Work-Out.

In the 1990s, GSA's Public Buildings Service had pioneered an event that served as the DNA for SLAMs. Named *Can't Beat GSA, it* was conceived to address a big problem. By law, government customers had been given more latitude to choose between GSA and other options for their real estate management. GSA needed to market itself and perform better in order to keep its business.

To that end, the Public Buildings Service brought together staff from around the nation, many of whom worked on similar (if not the same) projects but had never met each other. Together in a hotel conference room in Chicago, the group spent three days powering through sticky problems that had long hovered over the effective management of both the leased and owned portfolio.

In the room was a Table of Experts, which included the Inspector General, the General Counsel, and a representative from Human Resources, among others. If the group ran into legal, personnel, or audit obstacles, they consulted with the Table of Experts.

It was amazing to watch it unfold in the moment. The usual stalling ("We do not have the information," "Jack is not on board," "The lawyers will not approve") disappeared. In fact, they group solved so many problems that they felt confident to put even more on the table. Since all critical parties were together, it was a great opportunity to knock off other problems as well.

The *Can't Beat GSA* process had not been used during the Bush Administration, to my knowledge. When I returned to GSA I promptly reintroduced the notion, packaging it with the name SLAM. It caught on rapidly, but the label was actually a mistake. Ironically, we were moving so quickly to set up the first one that I used the wrong term. I had meant to say "SCRUM," because I was thinking of the way rugby players interlock to battle over claiming the ball. I was talking faster than I was thinking, however, and SLAM is what it became.

I described a SLAM as a blockbuster idea to tackle a messy problem by engaging a full circle of stakeholders in a room, on the clock, and with a lot of focus and support. It was, in addition, a technique for blasting past the lethargy and cynicism that chronic tough problems evoke.

I was soon delighted to hear that SLAMs were taking on lives of their own. Various groups inside GSA, eager for any process that could move their intractable problems, began organizing SLAMs almost immediately.

It may sound easy, but designing and facilitating a SLAM takes careful attention. A leader has to commission the SLAM, name the problem, and agree to move immediately on the decisions that emerge. The last point is probably the single most important precondition for a successful SLAM: the sponsor must have the juice to see it through after the event itself.

At GSA, attendees were expected to come to the event ready to share their ideas and knowledge and make decisions. Finance, human resources, operations, programs, legal, policy, oversight, and even customers were included to offer expertise, help generate options, and ultimately clear the final decisions. With all eyes on a problem, it was more likely that tripwires would be spotted.

Relevant information needed to be readily available, and even on hand. Attendees were to bring their phones, having alerted coworkers back at their offices that they might call them for missing data, information, or particular input. The "Phone Home Rule" was crucial to be sure we had no gaps.

Once everyone was in their seats with their coffee, nametags (we could never assume that all of the participants knew each other), technology, and materials, the leader(s) kicked off the meeting by stating the problem and expectations for solutions. They could excuse themselves after their charge, although they could also choose to stay, lending creative tension to the atmosphere that things had to happen.

Facilitators then stepped in. They laid out the problem more completely, posted an agenda, and started the (big) clock. At GSA SLAMs we would occasionally make a ceremony of locking the doors (fire codes obviously prevailed, so this was an entirely symbolic bit of theater). We would often pump up music at the breaks to keep the energy high. We posted big sheets of paper around the room so everyone could visibly track ideas and commitments. The agenda would designate a time for senior leaders to rejoin the SLAM, in order to hear what agreements and decisions had been made. Top management attention lent an element of pressure and expectation as well.

In short, the atmosphere and style of the SLAM were deliberately designed to be an exaggerated, whooped-up effort to focus everyone on solving a thorny problem within a finite time slot.

One particularly surprising problem arose during a few of the SLAMs. It was as if some participants found that the SLAM moved too quickly. A few participants did not or could not quite grasp that decisions were being made in the moment. They were not being obstructionists. Instead, it appeared to be something of an assimilation problem. Following months or even years of banging their heads over a problem, people could not adjust to the fact that solutions were actually getting agreement and approval. They were so used to petting a problem, working the politics, getting consensus, and shepherding a decision through approvals, that they met a solution or agreement with a sense of disbelief. How could the problem be put to bed? That just didn't happen!

To counter such response, we employed *agreement templates*, which were large preprinted or standard-language agreements with places for signatures and ribbons. Making a show and ceremony out of recording the decision and eliciting each participant's signature helped. Nevertheless, old habits were hard to break. It could take days and even weeks for people to blink their eyes, believe that a chronic problem had finally been addressed, and change their behavior.

Interestingly, most SLAMs I have attended have ended early. The careful design, leadership attention, materials, energy, concentration, fun overtones, serious undertones, and clock all seemed to galvanize decisions where none had seemed possible or available before.

The following are descriptions of three SLAMs for which I established and built out the process. The IT SLAM launched us and set the tone and template for future ones. The Hiring SLAM tackled a cross GSA issue in response to business needs. The FAR SLAM invited others from outside GSA to participate.

IT SLAM

When I left GSA in 2001, the agency was standing very tall. It had been one of the first federal agencies to extend internet access to all its employees. GSA was also a key player in creating the first web portal for the U.S. federal government, Firstgov.gov (now USA.gov).

When I returned to GSA in 2010, it was apparent that the agency's central information technology systems were dragging. We had lost our earlier edge and had significant operational needs. We needed to boost our ability to work remotely, assure proper security, work from the same software version, upgrade our phone systems, and build bandwidth capability.

The fact that the list of issues was a hodgepodge told me that we needed to find common energy and direction, as well as specific operational solutions. The idea of a SLAM fit perfectly. It required multiple layers of stakeholders, from technical people to users. It was even more important for GSA to get its groove back as a leader in innovative technologies. How could we possibly support government in modernizing, if we ourselves were behind the curve? We needed to regain our confidence.

The IT SLAM was my first as Administrator. It turned out to be a huge success and set the bar for future SLAMs. It was a little geeky in that it was created to solve a list of technical concerns. That made it all the more powerful. A good, collaborative meeting design could support decisions about complex and technical issues just fine. The facilitation team designed a host of creative processes that drew in everyone, educated many, and built real excitement and delight.

Importantly, the decisions made during the one-day SLAM radically revised the technology upgrade schedule. We were not going to wait for months or years to get some of the basic technology backbone upgraded and in place. As a result, we were ready much earlier to adopt cloud strategies, social networking capabilities, and better devices. GSA was back on the innovation map.

Hiring SLAM

Hiring people into government is complicated. I have been a recruiter in both the private and the nonprofit sector, and government hiring is, by far, the toughest. One reason is its sheer size. Applicants cannot figure out all of the options easily. Job categories and organizational charts are hard to understand from the outside.

A great deal of the difficulty in hiring, however, is due to the multiple players in the game: human resources, finance, security, line management, and the Office of Personnel Management. Some set the parameters and policies for hiring, while others do the actual work.

Within each of the different functions there are a host of rules and tasks. Assuring correct job descriptions, proper announcements, available budget money, sources of candidates, and fair reviews is governed by a great deal of procedure expected by the merit system. It seems that the more rules there are, the more it is that the people who are experts in the rules control the system, and everyone else becomes heavily dependent on those experts. That is the reality in government, for sure. Human resources, budget, and legal people all have to be in the mix in order to maneuver through the web of rules and process without missing a beat.

Tensions between managers and experts can become particularly high when the volume of work is up. GSA, at the time of the Hiring SLAM, had an aggressive strategy for building its brand, taking on new work and technologies, and market growth. There was a shortage of people, however. Retirements had been up, and hiring had been slowed both by budget uncertainties and the political uncertainty that came from not having a confirmed Administrator for two years.

Hiring was a perfect SLAM issue because it was more than a problem of efficiency. It was also about effectiveness—making extremely good decisions collectively. Getting the right people in place is, as every leader knows, the golden key to effective organizations.

A SLAM was also a good approach for this issue because a lot of tension—and even drama—comes with hiring new staff. Feelings run high. Managers have superhero hopes for candidates. Job descriptions try—and usually fail—to box such hopes into just the right words. Interviews are always a tough business because of nervousness that they will not be conducted with scrupulous fairness. Candidates write their resumes in the best possible light and then show up with normal-human-limp handshakes, shaky nerves, or hyped-up confidence. The entire process is fraught with possibilities for misunderstandings.

The Hiring SLAM did a good job of putting some steam into reducing our backlog. It also put the issue of trust on the table. Because hiring serves as the delivery room for an organization, stakeholders hold almost unreasonable expectations for the process. Thus communications and trust can become difficult. The SLAM, though fast-paced, provided an opportunity to hear from everyone. Using wall charts and "popcorn" sharing (quick, pop up and share your message with the full room), the SLAM invited everyone to participate. That had a surprisingly calming effect.

The Hiring SLAM was marked by very tough conversations in the room. Some felt isolated and under-appreciated in their work while others felt terribly under-resourced, strapped, and embarrassed that they could not provide needed support. Central and line authority competition was divisive. The facilitator worked hard to surface issues while paying attention to the level of complaining. Participants were not allowed to wallow in their woes, even though much had been pent up.

One particular solution was to find ways to run processes in parallel. Could stakeholders face the risk of doing their work, only to find possibly that it had been for naught? Would they feel put upon? Could they shrug and "take one for the team"? For example, was it worthwhile for one group to start processing candidates' security clearances, while another was still conducting interviews? Information from either process could derail a candidate. One person's work could pull the rug out from under another person's work.

The SLAM gave participants a forum to talk such scenarios out. It gave them a chance to surface and express a gracious attitude toward colleagues in service of getting the overall hiring job done. Could everyone find ways to bend and weave to improve the overall effort?

The Hiring SLAM resulted in noticeably expedited hiring in one major GSA division. The work acquired a blitz quality, with lots of senior attention and additional resources applied.

The lessons we learned, however, were both sobering and of more lasting value. We all walked away from that SLAM better able to dissect where the issues were systemic and the process was not our choice. The problems were not essentially interpersonal or intra-team. Outsiders dictated things like security clearances and job classification rules. Other pieces were within our control, but were lodged deep down in old habits and assumptions.

Each GSA SLAM raised the next question. Could there be a government-wide SLAM? We needed to do more to build awareness and credibility of the SLAM as a tool across government.

FAR SLAM

The Federal Acquisition Register (FAR) is a two-volume publication that lays out the policies for the government when it buys supplies and services. Its rules guiding both industry and government in their contracting activities are the framework for tens of billions of dollars of activity annually.

The complicated process of updating the FAR includes proposed rules, public comments, clearances, approvals, cross-checking, and setting the time sequence for changes against standing rules so that proper grandfathering and superseding occur. Because it governs contracts and is the first order of evidence in any contract litigation, the FAR language needs to be precise and clear in the extreme.

As a result, many stakeholders have a finger in the pie. Interagency panels and White House coordination are necessary. It is hardly surprising that changes to the FAR can take a very long time, with some adjustments taking years to conclude.

GSA's policy group is tasked with stewardship of the FAR. It is part of the small group that stamps changes and handles the administration of the changes. GSA was concerned that the backlog of proposed changes to the FAR had grown and grown. Perhaps holding a SLAM could help move things along.

Therefore, GSA invited representatives from the White House, the Department of Defense, that National Aeronautics and Space Administration (NASA), and other agencies to a FAR Backlog SLAM. Each participating organization has formal responsibility for reviewing and agreeing to changes in the acquisition policy process. DOD has unique acquisition needs, particularly in its development and deployment of weapons systems. And with a vast system of contractors, NASA has a challenging acquisition problem shared by many other government agencies.

The event took place in a large GSA conference room. The subdued hum in the room as people gathered illustrated one of the core challenges in government—many people who have similar responsibilities barely know each other. I opened the SLAM by welcoming people to GSA and explaining the goals. I emphasized the point that this was a chance for people to get acquainted. The facilitator further reinforced this by insisting on careful and complete formal introductions around the room, conducting an icebreaker exercise, and mixing and remixing work teams over the course of the day.

I left the room to its work, but during the day I thought about what was going on downstairs in that conference room. Each person attending played a part in the formal process for securing updates in contracting regulations, which affect a huge swath of our economy. Yet there seemed to be little sense of shared community.

It must be very difficult to do a networked job—in isolation. People must be very frustrated; I would be, if I were in their shoes. No wonder the FAR backlog had grown! I crossed my fingers that the magic of the SLAM could help solve not only the problem of the slow process, but also the human problem of loneliness. Could they build a sense of shared commitment, trust, and collaboration in a day?

When I returned at the end of the session for the formal report of results, the room was noticeably different. The noise level was way up, and bursts of laughter punctuated the air.

I joined a front table of leaders, including a White House representative, to hear what had been developed and was being suggested. We were given little cards, like the grading cards used on Dancing with the Stars, to register our response. Over and over, we all voted "4" (the highest score). The room erupted repeatedly in applause. There could be no doubt that the SLAM had made a big difference. The larger community was engaged with each other. A lot of underbrush had been cleared from the process.

The FAR Backlog SLAM demonstrated something that was pretty cool. Not only did it fix some historic problems, but it also bounced the ball into the future. In the weeks following the SLAM, the regulatory backlog seemed to shrink quickly. The SLAM had sped through some longstanding important items, as well as some stale lingering details. The effect was that everyone had a jump on the calendar and on the workload. For once, the contract regulations community had gotten at least a smidgen ahead of the curve. With the backlog cleared, the players experienced a sense of success they could apply to going forward. The SLAM had been a seed of energy that started an upward spiral of momentum and efficiency.

SLAMs do many things. They build community. They improve internal understanding and communications. They give people a sense that change is possible. They solve very sticky problems. They are a head start on the future. And they do it *fast*. Who could find fault with any of that?

I was delighted by how people embraced SLAMs and the results they produced. Instead of feeling it was always on me as the leader to push, nudge, steer, and wave flags, I saw peer solidarity unleashed. When people had a genuine, well-designed, specific, and time-bounded opportunity to work with colleagues on a common problem, they were able to steer themselves forward. By turning their eyes on the road ahead, they stopped watching each other. Longstanding misunderstandings and rivalries faded. More than once a participant whispered to me excitedly, "Can you believe they agreed to this?"

SLAMs also create an opportunity for leaders to be heroes. They can help organizations do what they were meant to do—

work together. But glory is not the main point. Trusting that one's organization can sprint once people have some techniques and tools is satisfaction itself.

Significantly, the press took notice of our GSA SLAMs. This was particularly interesting to me because a SLAM is a simple idea about how to conduct a meeting. It is about process, a subject usually too tedious for media coverage. Yet our efforts garnered attention. Here are links to a few articles:

http://www.federalnewsradio.com/697/1964979/GSA-SLAMs-its-IT-modernization-project

http://www.nextgov.com/technology-news/2010/08/gsa-slams-its-way-through-it-improvements/47294/

http://www.bizjournals.com/washington/print-edition/2011/02/11/gsa-hosts-a-slam-to-fix-acquisition.html?page=all

While we were designing, conducting, and learning to improve actual face-to-face SLAMs, we were also maturing a related idea: the virtual SLAM. The SLAM is a blockbuster idea being leveraged in the virtual world as well.

Online SLAMs or Ideation Events

We are now blessed with extraordinary *ideation* tools, which are online methods for inviting participants to contribute their expertise and ideas toward solving problems quickly. The notion is rooted in open sourcing methods for creating and improving software that have been popular for years. Now the tools are more refined and available to the non-tech lay community. They are, in many ways, an online SLAM.

I cannot think of anything in my recent career that has given me so much hope and sense of possibility. Ideation events are fast, often fun, and inclusive. They also solve problems! They come in many forms: contests and challenges, adjudicated processes (think about Wikipedia, with its rules and editorial boards), formally governed solution generation events, open source development, defined and facilitated Webinars, and more. There are also many tools, including e-bulletin boards, videoconferencing, and scheduling software, for simply connecting people.

I was introduced to these tools when I worked with a brilliant British colleague, Howard K. Smith, at the Computer Sciences Corporation. Together we tackled some prickly system-wide problems ranging from reducing accounts receivables on large projects to creating a strategy for sustainability. We explained this in an article, which you can find here:

http://assets1.csc.com/cscworld/downloads/9_CSC-WORLD_DEC08_IDEATION.pdf

When I reentered government in 2010, I was ready to encourage exactly the same efforts. It was a good time to do so. President Obama's agenda, new technologies, and the need for change were all coming together. Online collaboration was the emerging thing, and the government needed to take full advantage of it.

GSA was primed to play in this game. Its Office of Citizens Services and Innovative Technologies had been out front with collaborative online tools for a decade, starting with the first government web portal, now USA.gov.

It is hard not to be rhapsodic about what the government has been unleashing in this arena. Imagine posing problems to everyone in government or to the entire nation and receiving dozens, if not hundreds, of responses that can lead to new breakthrough options. Imagine encouraging online affinity groups—communities of people with shared interest and expertise—to help the government. Each of these efforts is a SLAM on steroids.

Intense innovation like this upsets many apple carts, unfolds unevenly, requires investment, and crowds into the spotlight. We all know that technology is disruptive, however, and what better to disrupt than some of the old stovepipe and rial habits of government?

The innovations sold themselves. My personal favorite was—and is—challenge.gov. GSA staff supported government agencies as they developed and posted problems and asked the entire nation for their best ideas, answers, and solutions. Many of the challenges were turbocharged by the promise of cash prizes. Below are some examples and more can be found at www.challenge.gov.

The Vehicle Stopper Challenge was sponsored by the Air Force Research Lab (AFRL). It launched a competition with a $25,000 prize for a viable, sustainable, and affordable means of stopping an uncooperative fleeing vehicle (small car or truck) without causing permanent damage to the vehicle or harming any of the occupants.

The challenge was so popular that it caught the attention of over 1000 problem solvers. 118 submissions came from 30 countries around the world. Dante Barbis, a retired engineer from Lima, Peru, suggested a novel solution for a device that is portable, inexpensive, and simple to operate. The AFRL team took the idea forward and created a working prototype in the hope of demonstrating a successful device to the Air Force Security Forces.

http://challenge.gov/AirForce/150-vehicle-stopper

The Million Hearts Risk Check Challenge was run by the Department of Health and Human Services, which posed the challenge of creating an application (app) that would support the Million Hearts™ campaign.

This was a national initiative to prevent one million heart attacks and strokes over five years. The first-prize winner was the "Heart Health Mobile" app, which teaches about heart disease risk and steers a person to close-to-home cholesterol and blood pressure screenings. The challenge yielded six winning apps for the government. Buying the services to develop those apps would have cost twice the amount of prize money awarded.

http://challenge.gov/ONC/398-the-million-hearts-risk-check-challenge

http://www.hhs.gov/news/press/2013pres/02/20130214a.html

Solar Flares was a NASA challenge (NASA has fielded over 40 challenges so far), which granted $30,000 for a breakthrough in forecasting solar flares

Fresh Food in Space was another NASA challenge. The winner received $11,000 in prize money for new methods to keep food fresh in space.

It is fantastic to explore the range of challenges that the government is asking the public for help to solve: How can we drop humanitarian food and water packages more safely? How can we build an anti-shredder that would reconstruct shredded documents? How can we promote better eating habits? The possible challenges are legion.

Experts and ideas can emerge from corners previously unknown and unimagined. More sophisticated eyes can surface possible solutions and assure fewer mistakes. The cycle of brainstorming and option development is shortened. We can surface a much richer set of options. And it can all happen zip fast.

I take great satisfaction that as these collaboration techniques were unfolding and taking root on my watch. I was able to be a proud sponsor, visible participant, and noisy cheerleader. GSA's mission is to help government be its best. SLAMs, both physical and virtual, will turbocharge government performance well into this century.

In Conclusion

Blockbuster ideas are precious. They help leaders transform an organization's worldview and from that change find new energy and creativity. Leaders cannot sit on the status quo. Yet for all kinds of reasons rooted in tradition, risk, and in-place inertia, the status quo is tough to take on. It requires powerful, supercharged, energetic, and innovative ideas to shift it.

Pull metrics, ZEF, the Workplace Revolution, and SLAMs were among the huge game changers I was able to champion at GSA. Each of them immediately engaged the workforce as well as the larger community that was involved in a problem. Each introduced a new way that blew through tired arguments and difficulties. Each captured people's imagination and powered a sense of creativity and possibility that led to substantive improvements. I am proud that they defined my leadership and will color my legacy.

PART TWO

WALKING THE PLANK

April 2, 2012, was exactly as miserable as I expected it to be. I printed my resignation letter to the President, signed and dispatched it, made my announcement to senior staff, and left. I took an elevator to the first floor and walked out the front door of GSA's headquarters. As I waved goodbye to the guards who had not yet heard the news, and as I looked for the last time at my portrait hanging in the lobby along with the President's, I felt numb.

In my statement to Congress during the two hearings held after my resignation, I said, "I will mourn the loss of this job for the rest of my life." Few statements could be truer.

The media and Congressional responses to the Inspector General's report and my resignation were as predicted. The storm was a real nor'easter, bearing down with a lot of noise, wind, and rain.

To be faithful to all who were touched by the events or impacted by their consequences, I want to emphasize that only a handful of the 13,000+ GSA employees were involved in the specific incidents, although we all felt the brunt of the storm. Furthermore, the money involved represented about 0.0009 percent of the funds that GSA channeled in the course of a fiscal year. The mistakes that had been made did not by any means characterize the norm at GSA.

There is no argument that there were mistakes—mistakes in judgment, contracting, and spending by public servants who knew better. In addition, the scandal occurred in the midst of the lengthy and ferocious Great Recession. Across the country, state and local governments under extreme financial duress were lay-ing-off workers and curtailing services. The federal government had tightened its belt. In that context, it was unconscionable that public servants at GSA were in any way profligate in their use of public funds.

As I said earlier, the scandal also occurred in a presiden-tial election year. The campaign was underway, and the two sides were already loaded for bear. Any chance to trip opponents, em-barrass them, or magnify their warts would not be passed up. A Las Vegas spending scandal promised at least a couple of news cycles of bluster and outrage. Both the traditional media and so-cial media were ready. When pictures and videos of the skits and spoofs at the conference went viral, GSA's credibility started to shred. Jon Stewart was totally funny; others were less than polite.

My job had been about inspiring an organization and de-livering value to our governmental customers day after day, week after week, and month after month. Regrettably, the month-after-month stuff cannot protect a leader from a very bad day.

∽

In this section, I offer two chapters that simply share the basic events and thoughts of those first days after I resigned from my position as Administrator. Looking back it was a whirl of decisions, conversations, hearings, and more. Time and events moved quickly and it bears taking a moment to remember and recount what unfolded.

CHAPTER FIVE

On My Watch

Even as I drove away from the office, once again a private citizen, the avalanche of concern from well-wishers was beginning. By the time I arrived home, emails, flowers, cards, wine, and phone calls were pouring in. Some of the messages expressed dismay and shock. Such sentiments were hardly surprising to me, given that I, too, was still absorbing the import of the situation. Others were supportive, recognizing the complexity of the moment, and noting that I was taking one for the team:

> I thought you might be able to use a note of friendship and encouragement.
>
> As an old Navy guy I understand the concept of the ship's Captain being responsible for everything that goes on below decks and the sense of accountability implied, but I also understand that organizations are a product of their long held cultures and tendencies. I suspect that many things were in flight when you took over, reflecting enormous organizational inertia. Changing behaviors in the short run is close to impossible.
>
> Unfortunately, this one had really bad optics.

Whatever the backstory, no matter how much change, overhaul, and good performance were in the mix, it had all happened on *my* watch.

Friends, colleagues, and especially people who have been in and around Washington politics or in a highly scrutinized corporate contretemps, could read the tea leaves. My resignation was not really about me, but about the institution. I resigned to help stop the public confidence in GSA from hemorrhaging.

I was a totem for an important organization that was chartered in the public trust, and my role as the leader was to stand publicly for the collective. I was the face of GSA. It was my picture that graced the website and hung in our lobbies across the country. I had been the one to channel or personify GSA's best. When it did wrong, justice had to be meted out. Fines, wrist slaps, restrictions, and limitations do some of the job of restoring justice. Beheadings make the point, too.

I also resigned, as everyone clearly understood, because I, too, had a captain. He was the President of the United States. He had placed faith in me by inviting me into his Administration. I had shouldered an aggressive and progressive agenda, because President Obama and his White House had an unusual understanding and expectation for GSA. The agency was viewed not just as an operational, but a strategic asset to government, and even the nation. As a result, we were involved in major progressive mandates ranging from sustainability and transparency to environmental justice, the Recovery Act, and more.

Who isn't loyal to a great boss? The job I had was very cool. It was an opportunity to make a big difference. The President did not want us to sit on our hands, hide in the corner, or come in through the kitchen. We were to get things done, change government, and by extension, improve the world.

Then, two years into the assignment, the question that had exploded in front of me was, "What happens if your organization has opened itself up for massive booing and jeering—in an election year?" Our errors with the Western Regions' Training Conference in Las Vegas were unfortunately ripe for loud ridicule. Right or wrong, inconsequential or substantial, fair or not, in an election year that noise counts.

As my friend said in his note, "Unfortunately, this one had really bad optics." He meant that the story of what happened would not be filtered through sympathetic lenses. Each grimy detail would be used to smear the Administration. Too many pieces were titillating. I resigned to foreshorten the story and turn down the noise. I was compelled to serve the welfare both of the agency and the Administration. My responsibilities did not only flow down to GSA; they also flowed up.

The Short Straw

Months after it all happened, I had coffee with a friend who is a corporate executive responsible for a large organization with billions in revenue. He was curious about the course of events during the spring and had waited for the dust to settle to get my full perspective.

Before I had finished the story, he clearly could not contain himself. "But, Martha, I have to interrupt you. To a leader like me, whether in government or not, there is nothing scarier than to hear a story like this."

He shifted in his chair and his voice went up a notch. "I've known you for years, and you were doing great stuff at GSA. This has been a damned horror show. If you, of all people, had to resign, how far away is the noose for any of us?"

Yes, frankly, the noose may not be far away from any leader. Both public and private organizations have all sorts of distortions, bad apples, twists, and turns, any one of which can become a career bender for a leader. Risk is part of the decor in the executive suite. The leader's name is on the door. The leader is the one on the hook. While others are responsible for specific actions and activities, the leader is accountable for the entire organization. Any leader who does not take that seriously is working in a fantasy office.

The responsibility and risk equation is complex. *It starts with personal behavior.* Leaders must conform to an exacting standard of ethics. Wrong behavior is just that. It invites and deserves direct punishment. Hands in the till, affairs with subordinates, personal corruption, and misrepresentation of knowledge are among the stories of downfall that have filled the media. There is a place for the wheels of justice to sort out instances of corruption, dissemblance, and violence against others. However, and importantly, that is not at issue here. Scandals caused by personal conduct are for someone else's book.

It moves to performance. Simply put, leaders are assessed based on the performance of the organization. While leaders have incomplete information, never enough time, and a host of other problems, the challenge is to optimize wherever possible, to make the organization more efficient and effective. Usually, assessment of a leader's performance can be done relatively dispassionately.

It includes accountability. Accountability comes in many forms, involving many shades of gray. Organizations are human systems. The people within them can do wrong, and those activities can fall along a sad continuum from the impolite, inappropriate, and ill-advised, through the unbecoming, unconscionable, and unethical, all the way to the criminal.

Accountability usually rises to the top when the actions have implications for the organization as a whole. This is not always an easy call or obvious, lying often as it does in the murky core of the:

- wrongdoing (from ignoring recycling rules for paper to hiding chemical waste that poisons groundwater)

- theft (from lifting a box of copier paper to skimming the books)

- processes/players that hid, did not see, or did not surface the malfeasance

- impact on customers and the market (from little impact to too-big-to-fail)

- clarity, possibility, and speed of a clean fix

- and more.

It is unclear where the Las Vegas conference story fits in the mix, and therein lies the banana peel of accountability. Regardless of specific tit-for-tat, the larger point is that accountability is contextual. Traders can squander millions in financial market jobs and not lose anything but a bonus, while ship captains shoulder responsibility and sometimes walk the plank for others' mistakes.

It lands on politics. When we received the Inspector General's draft report laying out his investigation into the Western Regions' Training Conference in Las Vegas, there was work to do. Many questions needed answering. What actions—both disciplinary and restorative—could I take? What new review processes did we need? Could I accept the IG report completely, or were there points that I should contest?

I set up a dedicated room near my cubicle for staff to read the report, look through the boxes of material that the IG had collected, and confirm facts. There was a lot of material from the 15-month investigation. I also had my own questions that had been triggered by the report. There was not much time.

I also met in a series of meetings with officials in the White House. They were necessary partners, because it was obvious that the report from the Inspector General was a public affairs bombshell that would blow plenty of dirt and shards right up Pennsylvania Avenue. Nevertheless, in more than one of those meetings, people said to me directly, "You are the one to decide what to do." GSA was, indeed, my agency and my responsibility. I had no doubt, however, that they were mightily concerned.

As we explored the report and our options, three channels of activity appeared in my mind. Disciplinary action was called for with respect to some employees. Corrective measures to systems and processes (reviews, authorities, and assignments) were necessary to prevent a repetition of the mistakes in the future. Finally, good communications, responding well to the inevitable questions, would be vital.

As I carried on with my full schedule of meetings, speeches, and travel, I kept tabs on the staff work and pondered what all of this could mean. Deep in my heart I had no doubt that the Inspector General's report, once public, would be a massive blow to the agency. I remember sitting on an airplane at one point, making long and deliberate notes about what GSA needed to learn and how I could lead them through those lessons. I started reading about organizations in crisis, turning points, guilt, shame, and recovery.

I never reached the point of putting those thoughts into action, because things accelerated. The impact of the *story* of the Las Vegas conference became more obviously damaging as more of the details emerged. The fact that the scandal was about contracting at GSA promised a shrill resonance. Since GSA was the *keeper of the contracting rules*, it was clearly even more egregious to break them. The standard was higher.

Consequently, GSA was an easy symbol for all-of-government decision-making and fiscal and contracting behavior. I was not solely the Administrator of GSA. I was part of a presidential administration in an election year.

As all of those angles emerged and swirled, I was asked to go to what would be my final meeting at the White House. At this fourth or fifth meeting called on the subject, the agenda was to be a final assessment of the situation with Jack Lew, the President's Chief of Staff.

That day I flew into Washington from a White House event I had been leading in Orlando, Florida. My Chief of Staff met me at the airport and went with me to the White House, where he waited for me in the reception area. When the meeting was over, I suggested to him that we walk for a bit before returning to the office. Absorbing my obvious tension, he was silent. When we got outside, I told him I was going to resign.

He was shocked. I was, too, frankly. I have always been able to turn on a dime if need be, but this was a weighty decision. The two of us walked aimlessly around a couple of blocks. We stopped for coffee but could not sit still. Our conversation was as undirected as our wanderings. He knew without my saying it that this was as hard for me as anything I had ever done in my life.

In Conclusion

As it turned out, there was no good answer. Printing and signing my resignation letter took barely a minute. It was short, to the point, and written for the public record. It was intended to be immediate, visible, and dramatic.

However, my resignation did not quell the noise. Well over a year later, the GSA Las Vegas conference still spawns reactions, new oversight policies and proposed laws, commentary in Congressional hearings, and media commentary. And, I still find my name in articles about scandals in the *Washington Post*.

CHAPTER SIX
After My Watch

When I said goodbye to my senior staff, I told them not to worry about me, but to get on with the business of taking GSA forward. I would be taking myself on a road trip. A few days later, my husband and I did just that, driving to Colorado so that I could visit my elderly father and decompress. Every mile we drove took the stress down a notch.

Thumb on the Bruise: Congressional Hearings

Unfortunately, just as we arrived in Colorado Springs my cell phone rang. A Congressional staffer on the line informed me that I was being called to appear at a hearing the next Monday. She wanted me to understand that the Committee had subpoena powers, just in case I was not entirely clear that they meant business with the request. It would behoove me to agree to appear.

Soon thereafter, I was requested to appear at a second hearing the day after the first.

It is never a simple or easy thing to be called before Congress, especially when the topic of the hearing is a report of mistakes and misdeeds. In my case, although I had left government and was a private citizen, I was still under scrutiny for matters in the government. The Congress, and particularly the Republicans, wanted the political benefit of showing their outrage about the scandal. I was in for a grilling.

I contacted a lawyer friend who has been in politics for many years. "You need a lawyer," she said, without giving me much time to finish explaining. "Not me, because I am not available. Let me make some calls." Within a couple of hours she was back to me with two names. "Either would be good. Both of them know the Hill and understand these things."

I called one of the names, and without missing a beat, he also said, "Yes, I've been following the story. You need a lawyer."

It was wise to have counsel along. At one of the two hearings where I eventually appeared as a witness, another witness, who had come by herself, was excused and strongly advised by the Committee Chair to seek counsel. It's not smart to go barefoot (that is, without a lawyer) when you appear before Congress.

There are a number of reasons for legal support. In my case, I had been the head of a massive, complicated agency. When I appeared before Congress, I had no access to my materials, because my schedule, files, and calendar were all government property. I could not check facts or reread materials to refresh or confirm my memory. A lawyer could help me wade through the situation of being under oath while answering questions that were both complicated and called on specific details that I could too easily confuse or blur. What date did I receive a memo? When did a meeting occur? Who was in the room? Cooperating *accurately* was the intention, but also a challenge.

A good Washington lawyer also helps by analyzing the intent and direction of the hearings, adding thoughts about potential questions, literally steering a client through the maze of rooms, fending off media, and sitting nearby during the hearing in order to advise, if necessary.

It would not be cheap to have legal support, but it was wise. Having made decisions on legal counsel, my husband and I got back in our car and started driving eastward. As he drove, I wrote one statement that I would file with both Congressional committees and a shorter version that I would read at the hearing. Late at night in a motel on Interstate 70, I struggled with the internet connection and was finally able to send my statement to my newly-hired-never-met-in-person lawyer.

We made it home in surprisingly good time. At 7:30 on the morning of the hearing, I arrived at my lawyer's offices to prepare. We set up in a conference room with big cups of coffee. He had already read my statement, but he started by asking me to lay it out for him. "Just tell it all to me." I started to talk.

At about 11:00 he ruffled through all of the notes he had been taking on a yellow legal pad. He looked at me, smiled, and said, "You know your truth. That's all you need to have with you. Let's have some lunch before we go to the Hill." It was spot-on, steadying advice, and off we went.

The hearings rooms were high ceiling affairs; the members of Congress were seated along two tiers of built-in desks above the witnesses. The media—there was a good cluster of people with cameras—were crowded into the space at the bottom of the tier in front of the witness tables.

The clicking of cameras coming from the well in front of the witnesses started the minute I entered the room and was more than a little distracting during the early part of the proceedings. Once they had their pictures and a sound bite, however, they disappeared, and soon we witnesses were left being watched by a stand-alone C-SPAN camera whirring at us.

Being seated with a handful of others from GSA made for an odd interpersonal experience. Some of the witnesses were both former colleagues and friends, but with cameras bearing down on us we held to ourselves. Even though it was necessary protocol, it was ludicrous to act in such a stony closed manner. As the hearing unfolded, however, I was enormously touched when the GSA witness next to me pushed his bottle of water over to me after I had drained mine. It was a small gesture that acknowledged we were all in this together.

All witnesses were sworn in at the same time. We were all questioned, some more than others. I was one of the main people quizzed. I had received a particular piece of curious advice about the hearings from a friend in the media. She told me that when I testified, I should not look directly at any of the members of Congress. "Don't look them in the eye, because doing so makes it more personal. You don't want that. This isn't about you, but about your office. Just look at the nameplates in front of them."

What a stunning bit of guidance! I thought it verged on gang protocol: do not look directly at the other guys unless and until you want to provoke. The advice, however, drove home to me that although the hearings were set up to be about fact-finding, they were also—and arguably largely—about politics and media. Committee members came and went during the hearings, some only appearing briefly to give their comments about their fury, outrage, and disgust at the events at GSA. For that matter, some of the members barely looked at me, talking instead directly to the cameras.

Months later I met a person at a going-away party for a mutual friend. "Oh, I remember seeing you on TV last spring," she said. "You were the red meat of the moment."

Among the lessons I took with me from the experience is the simple one of comportment. In the midst of pressure, hearings, and media attention, it works best to hang onto one's dignity. Holding it together, so to speak, gives form to a situation that seems to be crumbling. While others are shaken, someone needs to be the leader—and leadership does not end with resignation.

Frankly, I had no idea how I was appearing on the screen during the hearings. I only knew that it was the last time I could communicate with the organization that I cared so much about and from which I had been so abruptly yanked. Being calm and collected was important.

I was told later that GSA was a pretty quiet place during those hearings. Anyone who could manage it was watching from a desk computer or gathered in conference rooms with a big screen. Although at that witness table I felt alone and exposed, as one does in such situations, I still had an accumulated seven years with GSA. The bonds of hard work and partnership that I had enjoyed with many in the organization were not visible that day, but the hearings did not negate or devalue that shared memory.

Importantly, a witness in a hearing is not a defendant in a trial. I was not accused of anything. I did not need my husband or my pastor sitting behind me to look loyal and be supportive. All I needed to do was to be precise, answer questions, and avoid creating confusion. My lawyer was there to help me focus in the face of that task.

Hearings are intricate pieces of theater. While asking questions of me, many members took the opportunity to share their individual opinions about the situation. It was a moment to scold me and, by extension, to scold the agency. At one point I was berated for allowing a part of the GSA organization to perpetuate a culture of bullying. If anyone had asked me if I felt bullied right then, I would have said, "Yes."

On the Metro, on the way home after the second hearing, I was utterly exhausted, completely wrung out. I finally pulled myself together to check my phone messages. There was one from a former business colleague. "Just wanted you to know I watched the hearings, and you are one classy lady." Rarely have I appreciated a compliment more.

On the Street Where I Live

Then there is the matter of being on the evening news. The GSA story was in a media derecho, a severe storm system Washington area citizens know well. News organizations scrambled to talk about the IG's report, dig out collateral stories, or recycle the reports of others. GSA was the headline of the moment.

It was our 15 minutes of fame. Search my name on the internet and the screen floods with citations, articles, and YouTube videos from that time. There is a picture of me online with an arrow through my head. My personal favorite is *The Daily Show* clip during which Jon Stewart complained that not only did the government blow almost a million dollars, we blew it on lame b***s***.

Canteens, clowns, and bicycles? You're in Vegas! Unless those canteens were filled with cocaine ... you are a disgrace to corruption everywhere. I think I'm less upset about the waste of money than I am with the waste of opportunity.

GSA gave him so much material I am surprised he never sent me a thank-you note!

Some of it was funny, but none of it was fun. Frankly, I have checked Congressional hearings and media frenzy off my bucket list—permanently.

Luckily, only one satellite truck showed up in front of the house. When the reporter came to the door, my husband answered it and dispatched the lady firmly and promptly. About an hour later the truck drove off.

On the other hand, calls from all sorts of news organizations came in steadily. We simply quit answering the phone. My husband still tells people how astounded he was to get messages on his personal cell phone. "How did they find me? Do you know how many Steve Johnsons there are in the world?" Express packages containing letters on fancy network stationery arrived inviting me to appear on talk shows. I ignored or refused everything. I had no interest in continuing the story, for I had resigned in large part to shut it down.

As my son said to me later, "Everyone should have a brush with scandal, because you learn a lot about how to find and lose truth." It is sobering to be on the inside of a big news story. I was reminded for the umpteenth time that facts and tidbits can be tossed about, but context is astonishingly harder to convey.

I understand from friends in the media about the deadlines, financial pressures, and the changing demands of their markets. The result too often is provocative sound bites and little in the way of reporters and editors ready or available to unpack the full story. How can anyone extrapolate the story of an agency of such scale and complexity from the relative pinhole of a single conference and a handful of mistakes, all by the afternoon's deadline? It really can't be done.

Goodbye to Farewells

A leader's departure marks the end of an organizational chapter. Inevitably, people search for coherence, themes, and meaning to summarize that period of time. However long or short a leader's tenure, once concluded, it becomes part of the institution's history.

Leaving itself is not a casual moment. It can evoke sentimental, celebratory, difficult, or other intense—and often contradictory—emotions. Organizations can be unbalanced from losing their fulcrum, delighted to rid themselves of a difficult manager, or shocked and saddened at the demise of an admired boss. Leaders can be tired of it all and relieved to go, or ride out of town in a parade of goodwill and expectation for their next chapter.

When ties are severed, there is an opportunity for valuable, if at times painful, reflection and assessment. Coping with the ending can itself become a narrative that gets baked into the organization's history. Leaders and organizations often have to find ways to bring closure about the closure.

In my case, the transition was an unexpected jolt. The story of my leaving had the added drama of an abrupt event for which there had been little if any preparation. I learned a few life lessons in the process.

First, I was reminded about the value at times of simply staying in motion: it does no good to dither, stall, or second-guess when something dramatic is taking place. I did not have all of the information I needed, but I had enough. I did not have all of the time I wanted, but I had enough. I did not have all of the energy and bounce I wished for, but I had enough. There would be no benefit from combing, petting, or grooming the situation to ready it for prime time. Events were unfolding and I kept moving.

Second, ending my time at GSA as I did left me acutely aware of the value of various rituals that I had taken for granted my entire career. Specifically, I regret having no farewell ceremony to close the chapter that had started with formal ceremony.

There were no proper goodbyes. I did not have a chance to shake hands with people and tell them how much they had taught me and meant to me. I could not wish them well or hear them say goodbye. I did not get to eat any dry cake or laugh over stupid farewell jokes.

That sort of rending of the social fabric has been simply tragic to me. I was welcomed into the GSA community with enormous warmth, and even fanfare. I left in a slashing of bonds, with little chance to speak of the gratitude and appreciation I had for the organization and my colleagues. A brief resignation letter and a note to employees had to suffice, but they certainly did not do the job in such a complex, large community relationship.

Third, I recognized the value of the advice that when the time comes, leaders need to leave and get out of the way. The next leaders cannot do their jobs if the reality or the ghosts of previous leaders are hovering. An unwritten rule among the clergy acknowledges just that. It is respectful protocol when someone retires from a pulpit to avoid attending the same church for a couple of years. It is important to cut the cord, for lingering is confusing to everyone.

Lingering, however, is a funny thing these days. When I left GSA, I walked right out of the building and only briefly glanced up at the windows where the executive team was still meeting. At the time my departure seemed straightforward—a brief announcement and a rip-off-the-band-aid exit.

Since then, I have discovered that with social media, there are many avenues and connections that remain intact, presenting new protocols to consider. Do I "friend" GSA people? Do I accept their invitations? Who moves from the status of colleague to friend? Who is in my network? What is fair to me and to GSA? We all shudder at people who do not understand when it is over, and the chapter has ended. Their stories about the past sound dusty. How does severing organizational ties work now?

In Conclusion

It was over and then it was over again. Leaving office seemed a trailing affair and will continue to be so. The public process of hearings and media interest gave way to the personal process of thoughts and ruminations.

Much of the experience is the antithesis of a bucket list. None of it is was on my personal agenda of things I wanted to do in my life. Walking the plank, however, got me off the ship and into the water. From there I can swim in many directions, which I now turn to.

PART THREE

SURFACING

What next? The plank has been pulled back, and the ship has sailed away. How many movies have we watched in which the hero or heroine is deep underwater and clawing toward the bit of light above?

Since I left office, I have been surfacing. I did not blast to the surface to gulp the air in one dramatic whoosh. Instead, I repeatedly kicked my way up to the air, drawing deeper breaths each time, before sinking again below the water line. Ultimately, I trusted in my natural buoyancy. As I have worked at surfacing, I have become quite a powerful swimmer.

Compressing this part of my story into two chapters, I have chosen first to share a favorite of my resilience strategies—the use of surprise. Second, I have borrowed an idea from Warren Bennis and Robert Thomas about crucible events and their effects on leaders as a way to reflect on my own experience.

CHAPTER SEVEN
The Strategy of Surprise

I have two children who are both adults now. When they were little tykes, they would have various accidents, such as crashing a bike or falling off playground equipment. Some parents have the following rule: "If there is no blood, we will not worry." My reaction when my children came crying was, "Are you hurt, or are you surprised?"

My question, if a little unusual, was a legitimate one. Of course they were hurt. I could see that. I asked the question as an "either/or" to get their attention. I would take care of the scraped knee or palm, but we would also talk about another way to describe what they were feeling. How could they narrate the story of their little catastrophe? What could they take from the experience? Could they learn to describe their situation even as they were in the throes of it? I wanted them to have such skills because I believe they help in recovery well beyond iodine, band-aids, and hugs.

The question is good for adults, too. Life is full of scraped skin, broken windows, crashed hard drives, returned engagement rings, and flat tires. Usually we are caught up in a mix of emotions: foolishness, pain, annoyance, and disconcertion. What about surprise? It can often be a good thing—even wonderful. A finger snap wakes a person up. A little jolt of surprise fuels jokes. Surprise parties are treated with glee and long remembered.

Surprise is defined by Webster's as "a taking unawares, or a suddenly excited feeling of wonder or astonishment." *Wonder and astonishment* are part of the marvels of life. They invite a dollop of awkwardness, a slight shift in our worldview, or a compelling delight in something new.

Granted, surprise probably comes best in bite-size chunks. There can be such a thing as too much wonder and astonishment. Being surprised when an asteroid slams into the roof of the car evokes wonder and astonishment. It also evokes fear, anxiety, damage, and cost. That constitutes shock more accurately than surprise.

Nevertheless, even with shocks we still ask questions. "How can that have happened?" "Can you run that tape again?" The tight constructs of life loosen. New possibilities are suddenly... well ... possible. Our worldview opens, if only a flicker. As a result, people can learn, discover, grow, and generate new energy for life.

People are riveted by stories of setbacks that turn into comebacks. War fighters lose limbs in combat but rebuild their lives and run marathons. Crops fail as soil erodes in windstorms, but farmers find ways to restore and reclaim their lands. Most of the time, such stories are laced with determination, stamina, and persistence. But is that always the case? Is resilience necessarily only about all of that grit or those super-human goals?

My response is a *yes, and* .... Times of trouble require rebuilding, which is very hard work. However, we needn't shut the curtains on another source of light and energy. Glimmers of *wonder and astonishment* must be allowed to shine in as well. No matter how small or fragile, the element of surprise in any disaster offers a window onto new possibilities.

Treasure Surprises

I found the simple little question of hurt vs. surprise helpful in the first days after my resignation. On one level there was the sheer shock of the thing. One week I was leading a massive organization focused on vital issues, and the next week found me looking at the dust on the furniture.

It was, however, also a time of great surprise. In spotting glimmers of wonder and astonishment in those first confused days, I realized I had not completely emptied my bank of spirit and humor. I recognized signs of ways to move forward.

What Were My Surprises?

First, I was surprised to have free time. It was a luxury I could not remember having since childhood, and I almost could not believe it. I could sleep. I could talk to my husband. I could exercise. I could read a book from cover to cover. At times I would catch myself looking at the clock and thinking about my former workday schedules. "Are they in the staff meeting? Where would I be now if I were at GSA?" And then I would look around the local neighborhood bistro, open a magazine, and become absorbed in the article at hand.

Second, I was surprised by my children's deep interest in what was going on. They cared about me, of course, and were upset on my behalf, but they also wanted to figure out what had happened. They watched the news, the political comedy shows, and the hearings. They called and wanted to talk through various pieces. What a surprise not only to have a place to talk about the events and work through them, but also to do it in a way that was a gift for someone else! As they asked, probed, combed, and learned, so did I.

Third, I was surprised by my sense of relief. The job had been a hard one. Let someone else meet with that unreasonable senator. Let someone else worry about the renovation of the White House. I was surprised at how my responsible self was happy to take a vacation. Maybe I was not such an incorrigible workaholic, after all!

These surprises among others gave me new energy. They worked to knit me back together in ways I could not have anticipated.

Become the Surprise

The first function of surprise is to see that *wonder and astonishment* can be teased out of a disaster. Searching for the surprises provided me early on with a little methodology for sorting through the experience of my resignation.

Surprise doesn't stop there, however. In addition to being surprised, I could *become* the surprise. By doing something unexpected, I could shift my game. Most importantly, becoming a surprise gave me new firing rockets and not a small amount of glee.

There are many examples of people becoming a surprise as one phase of their lives ends and they enter another. After her marriage fell apart, Sarah, the Duchess of York, wrote the *Budgie the Little Helicopter* series and became a spokesperson for Weight Watchers. President John Quincy Adams, upon losing the 1828 election, made a U-turn and became a Congressman. After years as a pro football player, Rosie Grier did a lot of things, not the least of which was publishing a book on needlepointing. President George W. Bush has taken up painting.

After my resignation, I dug into a project I had been nursing for years. I had been writing a novel while riding the commuter bus to and from Washington. I had a solid manuscript already in hand. Suddenly, I had uninterrupted days in which to polish and finish it.

I had a ball. I wrote and rewrote, enjoying the refuge, fantasy, emotion, and fictional friends. At the end of the summer, I went into production, nailing a cover design, a website, and various distribution outlets. In September of 2012, I published *In Our Midst*. It was delicious!

A friend says gently, "Oh, Martha, I've been thinking about you. I'm so sorry about what happened. I hope you are able to find some peace and move on."

"Thank you," I reply. "It was a difficult period, but things are going well. As a matter of fact, I just published a novel."

Pause.

"A novel? Really! Wow! That's amazing. I hope it's about a gruesome, politically motivated murder in Washington."

"No," I say. "Actually, it's about gay teen suicide."

Pause. (Longer.)

I cannot deny it. Every time I had that conversation, I felt better.

In Conclusion

Bit by bit, the surprise strategy worked its charm for me. Just as with every other major event that has affected my life, there have been phases of adjustment. Each has the initial jolt of surprise, now that I understand to look for it. Its energy is that extra kick that has helped me get up in the morning and take on the new day.

CHAPTER EIGHT
My Crucible Experience

I fell off a train once. It was 1975, outside Ayutthaya, Thailand, early in the morning. My friend and I were enjoying tea in our seats and watching the scenery go by. On school break from our university teaching in Taiwan, we had caught the overnight train out of Chiang Mai where we had been touring temples and night markets.

The train stopped. It appeared we were in the middle of a rice field. We continued to sip our tea, trying to avoid drinking the floating tea leaves. As the train lurched back into motion, the conductor rushed up the aisle, "Ayutthaya!" We had missed our stop.

We grabbed our bags, and Josephine headed to the door. The train was picking up speed. She was wearing high heels (don't ask; we were 24 years old). The conductor was at the door pointing, "Ayutthaya." Josephine flung herself out the door onto the banks of the rice paddy.

As I watched her land gracefully, I stumbled, and out I went, landing not so gracefully in the spongy dirt and barely missing the rush of the train wheels. In a manner of seconds, the train had passed. We were in Ayutthaya and I was alive, but when I tried to stand up, I realized I had smashed up my ankle.

Crashes, falls, and slams into walls are part of everyone's life story. My fall from the train resolved itself with a cast and crutches. I hobbled for six weeks. Losing my position as the Administrator of GSA required much more. It had been a grand sweep: I had lost my job, my title, my government career, and many longstanding colleagues, as well as the daily schedule and activities that had structured most of my life. I had also lost a platform from which I had hoped to make a big difference for a lot of people, for the environment, and for my nation. I had been on a mission, and it had been somehow yanked away. I was in a blur of confusion about how in the name of heaven this had happened to me.

All of the other crises I had been through until then had been highly personal. I had fallen off the Thai train, had a miscarriage, lost friends to cancer, and lost money on a house. My father had been nearly blinded by surgery. None of that, however, had prepared me for a major loss in full, front-page, public view. It was a trauma done up in the trailing black ribbons and bows of headlines and hearings.

It was also a redefining experience. My life had suddenly turned 180 degrees. I felt professional and emotional whiplash. I was back at the basics piecing them, like a damaged Lego castle, together again. In the professional literature, this is called a crucible experience, and it is credited with particular importance for leaders (see *Geeks and Geezers* by Warren G. Bennis and Robert J. Thomas).

For a time, I hardly thought of the experience as a leadership thing. It was simply a loss for me, and in those early days it was everything to me. When a person breaks a leg, it does not matter how many others have had the same experience. My "leg" hurt, and it hurt badly. Sleeping was tough. Conversations were awkward. Friends didn't want to pry but were curious about the politics. I couldn't escape the story. People at the next table in a coffee shop exclaimed over "those lazy government workers having a party in Las Vegas."

Surfacing was a slow process. It was also inexorable. Things did begin to change. The chatter dwindled or pricked differently. A friend took us to the beach and the waves were a wonderful new sound in my head. Bit by bit my thoughts, attitude, and spirit shifted to become more about tomorrow than yesterday.

There was no straight line about the shift, however. Three months after the events, I had a panic attack. I suddenly doubled over and was not completely sure I could breathe—not my usual style. Yet I was also already outlining a book and learning to swim. Four steps forward, two strides sideways, a couple of slips backward. One thing was for sure. Every succeeding day was slightly different.

Frankly, I struggled to see the point in the whole thing. What was it people said about fate, about the random bumper cars of life? Was there something here to be learned? Was there some useful purpose to be divined? As it turned out, the answer was—and continues to be—yes. My crucible experience had bashed me up, and it had also bashed open some windows into myself. I was bruised, but I could see into myself more directly.

My insights took hold at their own bidding. I could not stamp my feet and make the surfacing process happen to my beat. It is absolutely true that you can't sleep fast. I had to be patient and allow the process to unfold and do its work. While events may happen in a snap, absorbing their lessons does not follow a structured schedule. I once heard an artist talk about the value of seeing a contemporary art exhibit, while cautioning that the viewer might not understand its full value for years to come. How right she was!

Insights also emerged in syncopation. Banal observations and life-changing wisdom showed up at random times, without relationship to each other. It was like living a life of downbeats and offbeats without a score. All in all, it added up to a veritable symphony of new awareness about myself and, yes, about being a leader.

The latter awareness was particularly interesting, because for a time I was not sure why it was worth discovering wisdom about leadership. What good would it do? I no longer had a platform or a vast organization with which to put that wisdom into practice. Or did I?

Chapters from My Crucible Primer

Leadership is not just about particular positional status. It is not something to turn on or off. It is a form of maturity that infuses one's life. As it happened, the leadership insights that my crucible experience offered were of significant value to me personally. They could also be helpful to other leaders who are surfacing after a setback or a blown-up course. I could not round out a book about leadership without sharing some of my insights.

The First Round of Chatter Kicks In

Sympathy cards are a good place to start. I received many. The world is full of advice and tough love for the shattered. I quickly learned of an industry out there ready to greet me. It started with the bumper sticker platitudes that arrived in the mail, accompanied packages, or laced the daily horoscope:

- Pour yourself a drink, put on some lipstick and pull yourself together. —Elizabeth Taylor

- Someone I loved gave me a box full of darkness. It took me years to realize that this, too, was a gift. —Mary Oliver

- Everything will be OK in the end. If it's not OK, it's not the end. —Popularized in the movie, *The Best Exotic Marigold Hotel*

- We must be willing to let go of the life we have planned, so as to have the life that is waiting for us. —Joseph Campbell

- Don't cry because it's over, smile because it happened. — Attributed to Dr. Seuss

- It's not the strongest of the species that survives, nor the most intelligent that survives. It is the one that is the most adaptable to change. —Charles Darwin

- You can't always get what you want, but if you try sometime, you find you get what you need. —Mick Jagger and Keith Richards

The messages moved on to yoga tapes about relaxing and resume services for those interested in reinventing themselves. There were—and still are—coffee dates with others in Washington who have fallen on swords, as well as an unending sequence of conversations with people offering advice and sympathy. At the outset, I was quite a busy person. Moving on was at first a lot about moving around.

Networks

My network was a godsend. Not only was it surprisingly and remarkably extensive, but it really came through. Along with truckloads of sympathy, it offered real support—financial, legal, professional, spiritual, practical, and political.

If I have one bit of gratuitous advice to give to anyone, it is that leaders need networks. And, as a corollary, you cannot build them when you need them. This is not a just-in-time proposition. Networks have to be part of the equation at all times. Going it alone is not just a silly Rambo fantasy, but it is also foolish.

Interestingly, I believe my network wanted to be involved and reached out to me not just for the sake of the individual connection. My very public demise made it a part of others' lives as well. They had their own adjustments and understanding to achieve—about me, about the Administration, and even though it sounds grandiose, about our collective political life.

I represented a direct and personal line into the larger world of governance and politics, which people track daily through the news. I was a totem, a living example whom they could touch, and whose personal story they cared about. I had been in the midst of public life, and a surprising number of people grabbed at their connection to me in order to understand the larger flow of events that they regularly followed and studied.

The Saddle

When a crisis hits, the advice a person hears is to get back in the saddle. Whatever the fall or dustup, put a foot in the stirrup and swing back up. The point is to prevent residual fear or inhibition from making moving forward too hard. Shoulders up, face forward.

I advise caution. My own first reaction on losing my job was to head right out and find another one. I pounded out a resume, found the email addresses of references, spent money on getting good job listings, and set up meetings with all sorts of people to track opportunities. It was all reasonable activity. I had counseled many on how to find a job and knew the ropes. It was too quick, however.

While I needed to find an income, I also needed to take a breath and think about what made sense. Did I want another intense, large, executive job? Had I truly assimilated what I had learned in the last one? Why was I assuming that more of the same was the right answer, or, in fact, the right next expression of my leadership? Why should I believe that with such a crash just behind me, I could charge forward as if nothing happened?

Back in the saddle is not the only answer. In fact, it can be the wrong one. Remounting the horse might be fine for recovering some muscle memory quickly, but it might not necessarily be the long-term answer. The hardest lesson I had to learn was patience.

Old Tapes

I do not think people can predict their reactions when a crisis hits. In fact, speculation can be a bit of a parlor game. Would I prefer fire or ice? Would I come up punching or turn into a puddle on the ground?

In the wake of my demise as GSA's Administrator, I found myself afraid. It was a raw fear, more than I had felt at any other time in my adulthood. It was clearly sparked by the public nature of the experience and the massive attention it attracted. There was a mob feeling about it that was deeply scary.

Fear is a very old tape for me, as I am sure it is for many. It has its roots in my childhood. As the daughter of a minister, I learned early on that my family was always on display. All eyes were on us, on me. If I ever stepped out of line, I could put my dad's job in jeopardy, our house on the block, and who knows what else. Believe me when I say that I took that childhood fear into my heart.

In the course of my very public resignation, it was hardly surprising that the old fear reappeared. The press attention set off emotional alarm bells. My stomach knotted up when the phone rang. I could not bring myself to answer the door when the media truck was out front.

I knew rationally what was happening to me. I had worked with the media before in many a thoughtful interview. The turn in my confidence happened because I was suddenly faced with the worst version of my childhood scenario. Even without misbehaving, I was losing my job. The younger Martha's overwrought fear was turning into an adult Martha's reality. Scary stuff was happening that I did not and could not control.

It took effort and concentration to convince myself over my pounding heart that I was not finished. My family might be confused, more than a little miffed, and sad for me, but we were not about to lose our health or home. I was under scrutiny, but I was crystal clear about who I was and I wrote my statement for Congress basically in one sitting. Each time I shivered, I made myself stare down the situation once again.

Fear is a tenacious beast. The huge bust-up that became my crucible event created an opportunity to see right into its very center. It was time to do some emotional cleanup. It took awhile, but eventually the shivers disappeared. There was no longer any reason to cringe behind 50-year-old fears.

From "What if?" to "How To"

Could I have changed the outcome if I had been smarter about politics?

I have never claimed to be a politician. I don't know that I could have anticipated what led to my stepping down. Perhaps my senses were dulled by the 15 months we waited for the IG report. Perhaps I believed that since I was traveling and speaking for the White House, they trusted and valued me more than turned out to be the case. Perhaps the thorough surprise of my circle of astute political staff clues me in that I was not alone in my naiveté.

The "what-if" questions can be unending. Perhaps I did not appreciate the extent of White House nervousness in an election year, because I had never been on a campaign. Perhaps my years of experience with the peccadillos and bizarre things that organizations can serve up had confused my calibration of indignation. Or perhaps having no experience of a scandal before, I did not recognize the phases of acceleration.

While these are valid questions that I have worked to answer, I find them ultimately to be circular.

One question did lead me forward. I asked myself about my fighter instincts. Did I fight hard enough for myself and for GSA? Or, have I watched so many heroic movies of people taking last stands that the romance of the idea likes to shake its finger at me?

I know I do not like open combat. I am more of a passive-aggressive fighter than a fists-up type. I lived out that tendency as I stepped down. It's who I am.

A big lesson for me is that I *did* turn my anger inward. I dismissed it, ignored it, and avoided it, but it sat there holding me down and depressing my core. It has taken months of tiptoeing, zigzagging, and do-si-doing to regain a sense of confidence, that shake-of- the-head feeling that I am free again. The first version of this book featured a highly sanitized discussion of a leader's compass of needed strengths. Huh? My editor howled with laughter and said perhaps that could be my second book, but first I needed to "pass go" by digging into and then telling the GSA story.

The ultimate takeaway has been the how. How have I expelled my anger, incorporated the experience without a new layer of protective fat, and rebuilt my muscles of joy? Yes, it has been in the story telling. Yes, it has been in the passage of time. Mostly, it has come from the discipline of my writing, and that has been very satisfying to recognize.

It happens this way. My brain spins words or sometimes ideas. Phrases come together in my head as if I am imagining a person saying a string of words, mimicking a speaker, preaching, or satirizing. I think this comes from my fiction writing. It is about inventing characters and letting them talk.

I write the words down. They do not speak of a reality, but they are on the screen—captured, so to speak. They are very simple—a fragment of a thought, a string of words, a metaphor—and I leave them there. I continue to write.

Eventually I come back to edit, move, cancel, embellish. I work over an idea, twisting it and connecting it to others. Sometimes I string seven or eight ideas together and then turn on them and delete the entire collection, because that road is not leading me anywhere. At times it has no light at the end of it, or I am caught in a maze. At other times I can tell the ideas are confirming each other. The south and west trails triangulate and confirm what is north and east. They are true, and I have found another roadmap that directs me somewhere. My excitement about the journey builds. The bounce emerges and the joy returns.

Living Out Loud

I am not under 40, but instead over 60. I am in the demographic of people who tiptoe up to their computers and fret over social networking. In conversation with friends, I often hear laments over the loss of privacy and the lack of inhibition of the younger generation who post pictures online of their breakfast toast and the new puppy wearing dark glasses. It is called *living out loud,* and many of my generation struggle to understand it. Some scorn it completely by refusing to be on Facebook or otherwise face up to the Twitter feed.

Here is one dilemma I do not have to fret over. I have no choice. My name and pictures are already all over the internet.

Both my signing in and signing out of public service made news, so the library of online postings about me contains a telescoped version of a couple of days in my life repeated across all the channels. It is a done deal. I am on the other side of the 15 minutes of fame thing. I am already out there for all to see. I have joined the younger generation.

Grit

I know now that before all of this happened, I did not have as finely calibrated a sense of people as I thought I did. I always felt I could read people to sense their moods and hidden agendas, and I had some good evidence to that end. I wasn't a clod about assessing others, but I can tell now that I missed a lot.

As I faced down my resignation and the subsequent upheaval in my life, I had many hard conversations with myself about what my life and work were all about. Hard, yes, but not scraping bottom. No one had died. I was hardly at my wit's end. If anything, I had reserves I had never tapped or even known about. I had in me a lot more stretch before the rubber band would snap.

All of this meant that while I may have been able to read people in the past, I didn't have much imagination about what their inner resources were. This isn't very surprising, since I had not yet really tapped or plumbed my own. The outcome now is that I can see more into and about people. I recognize that they are less fragile than I once believed. I have been through something that tells me that others are much stronger than they appear—or perhaps even know. I am less inclined to make excuses for others. I put more chips on the table, and I know they can, too.

What Would I Do Differently?

When I give speeches these days, I inevitably get the question, "If you could do it over, what would you do differently?" My answer is in three parts. First, there is no way I could lose such a great opportunity and position without asking that very question every day for months afterward. Could I have prevented it from happening? Could I have changed the outcome?

While I tip my hat to the idea that one should embrace the lessons of experience, my response to those questions is, frankly, no. The GSA environment was a grinding machine of activity, decisions, and fast-moving events. I believe I did my very best. To second-guess that now would be to wallow in undeserved personal recrimination. I simply will not do that.

Second, I prefer to shift the question. If I were in a time machine that put me back in the old swirl equipped with what I know now, there are some things that I would *not* do. I would *not* choose to be more controlling or micromanaging. I would *not* in hindsight assume the role of playing cop. Gripping harder to the steering wheel would neither have prevented the events leading to my job loss nor steered me better; nor would micromanaging have been good for me or the agency's performance as a whole.

Third, and most importantly, I would ask a very different question: How would I *think* differently, if I had it to do over? That question is at the core of one's leadership philosophy and can unpack valuable lessons.

My answer to *that* question involves the seminal leadership issue of trust. If I had to do it over, I would think differently about trust. If I knew then what I know now, I would understand that trusting people in the GSA organization was a greater leadership gift than I ever appreciated.

Let me explain that a bit more: I lost a major position as a result of organizational arrogance, with garden-variety missteps that were badly timed and naively juvenile. It was enough to send me around the bend in frustration. I had put my trust in people who then abused it.

It is the simple humanity of the mistakes, however, that is at the heart of this story for me. People are people. We are all frail, prone to bad habits, vanities, and imperfections. As the warts appear, and they inevitably will, a leader has to continue to extend trust. Leaders are not—and never will be—leading a choir of saints. That cannot be a precondition for a leader. Leaders lead people, and people are human.

Importantly, leaders always have to go first. I had to trust GSA, or it would not have ever trusted me back. Trust and human frailty had to and will always do their dance. Given what I know now, leadership trust is altogether more poignant, valuable, and *necessary*.

Enthusiasm

Ralph Waldo Emerson once said, "Nothing great was ever achieved without enthusiasm." How very true, and how particularly true about me!

Enthusiasm is my hallmark, and it was important to me as a leader. Blockbuster ideas need enthusiastic champions. Leading under oath requires patriotism and an enthusiasm for the public square. Enthusiasm fuels a leader through the anxiety of leading in the dark and leading at scale. Importantly, *enthusiasm for oneself* is the propellant for leader heading into a next phase. Leaders use enthusiasm to sustain themselves through life's chapters as well as to galvanize organizations for important challenges.

The great enthusiasm I brought to GSA was a choice, but it was not hard to make. I prefer to be enthusiastic. I am naturally positive, believing good things are within reach. Organizations are desperate for a lively and positive leader. It is an important antidote to the oversupply of bureaucracy and traditional caution already embedded in most systems.

Not everyone appreciated my enthusiasm, of course. Some thought I was naïve and less than properly suspicious of the snakes in the organization. My glasses were shaded too pink. Some told me so directly, while others whispered it out of my hearing. "That Martha Johnson is a little over the top."

Yes, leaders of large bureaucracies are expected to be measured and deliberate. Boring is considered safe and nonthreatening. However, it was not abundant enthusiasm that put me in jeopardy or brought about my resignation. Had I been boring, I am certain the same thing would have happened. For my money, therefore, Emerson is the man. Enthusiasm was my gift to GSA. If they would have me as a leader, I would believe in them lavishly.

Having stepped away from the fray, I have wondered about my enthusiasm swish. What is it really about? During the surfacing phase, I have called it up, but I have had to fake it in some cases. "Yep, doing well. Talking to folks. Coming up with new ideas. Busier than ever." I still had a store of natural enthusiasm, but it needed brushing off and straightening up.

I am learning that my genuine and signature enthusiasm is not about cheerleading. I have used it that way in all of my jobs. I used it to project confidence. It was loud and hearty, and that was natural since I was blessed with a strong set of pipes. Now, however, my enthusiasm is less about *projecting* confidence and more about *offering* confidence. It requires of me a kind of bravery, because it is less about controlling others (forcing the positive on them) and more about bearing witness to my beliefs (being honestly positive). Surfacing has had a quieting effect on me, because the bluster is out of me and the audience is different. My enthusiasm is now effectively more genuine.

Normal Can Become Remarkable

Without the mad rush to and in Washington, my life is very different. Family and friends have told me for years that I should slow down and smell the flowers. Now I can, and I do.

It is hardly a surprise that my life is now more rounded with a complement of such activities as singing, quilting, and travel. What interests me is that these activities are not hobbies that fill my time, but they are instead becoming a deeper means of expanding my life. In the maze of planning a quilt and working through color theory, I now find special metaphors in the scattering of dark and light triangles or the juxtaposition of the squiggly and the stark fabric patterns. Contrasts are not something to toss off willy-nilly. Neither is it easy to place various shades of blue in the right sequencing. My sensibilities are more acutely tuned with every seam.

Ten months after resigning, I found myself organizing an event called a Weekend of Prayer to End Human Trafficking. Sponsored by my church congregation, it was intended to raise awareness of the issue and its presence here in the state of Maryland. I found movies, ordered books, collected posters, and learned about pending legislation. As we planned, I decided we also needed to embed the information in a deeper way. In order to come to grips with the problem, we had to relate to it in more dimensions than factual briefings.

As a result, I asked another committee member to make a tableau representing the tiny room of a sex-trafficked girl who is confined and expected to service clients. As Elizabeth created and "decorated" the tableau in a closet in the church, I set up tables nearby as a workspace. I had put out a call for chains and nail polish and had collected a fair stash. People were invited to sit down and paint the chains with the polish. From where we sat, we could see the padlock on the door into the tableau. As we worked, the fumes from our little bottles were powerful. The chains slowly turned hot pink and sparkling orange, at once ugly and glossy. Eventually, we draped them over pews in the sanctuary for the Sunday worship service, where they provided stark witness to the issue.

The tableau and the chains embedded themselves in us. The event informed people about the facts, but it also conveyed on a different level the reality and horror of the problem. The hours spent making those tiny brushstrokes of paint on top of rusty iron pushed me personally into more clarity about what is important, what is truly dangerous, and what is possible.

Artistic activities are precious beyond measure. To have new emotional elasticity is part of my story of surfacing. It is extraordinary to be finding new forms of expression. I can see in the process that I have powerful skills in leading people to new awareness. I am truly able to *move them.* When I had leadership jobs, I urged organizations to be creative and to find creative solutions. It is only now that I fully grasp how my own creativity makes me a leader.

In Conclusion

My crucible event and its aftermath have better anchored me in life's choppy seas and added definition to my identity as a leader. A year ago I would have written a cheery, I-Am-Woman article without much irony and talked about getting the next executive job fast. Now, as I sip coffee from my bone china mug, I think and write about leveraging creativity and recognize that I am embarking on the next 20 years of possibilities.

Lead, leave, learn, and lead again.

ABOUT THE AUTHOR:
WHO IS MARTHA JOHNSON?

You, the reader, probably do not know much about me. Allow me to establish a bit of a baseline for you. Leaders learn from one another, and you probably want to size me up so as to calibrate the advice I am sharing. Fair enough.

I come from a strong-minded, socially liberal clan. Various ancestors were activist clergy. They include a circuit rider minister, missionaries to Japan and Appalachia, and a founder of an orphanage. My father was a parish minister, and I grew up in the parsonage.

When I was in the fourth grade, the free speech movement at the University of California at Berkley was unfolding literally down the road. At the dinner table, my father declared the event would change my life. He believed in teaching us about the problems of the world. He once took me out of school to hear Cesar Chavez testify before Robert Kennedy's Sub-Committee investigating the plight of migrant workers. It was my first glimpse of a Congressional hearing in action.

Dad's edgy preaching contributed to his being pressured out of his pulpit in California. So, we packed up and moved to North Dakota. There he served a congregation and founded a still-flourishing environmental advocacy group. I absorbed the important lesson that losing a job is hardly the end of the world. In fact, it takes a person to a whole new world.

My mother was a musician, artist, and master teacher. My earliest memories are singing in her choirs. Blending voices was important. Much later, in the middle of the feminist movement at college, I was not at all sure if being assertive was the right goal. To me it meant a diva artistic personality. I did get one thing clear from singing, and that was a sense of the exquisitely honed beauty of teamwork.

As a frugal minister's wife, Mom knew her domestic arts, and so therefore do I. Our house was a constant *art* studio. To this day I look for the prism that will shoot some color or flourish into an issue, a meeting, a speech, or an assignment.

As a preacher's kid from North Dakota, I was a good bet for scholarships, and off I went at age 16 to boarding school, then Oberlin College, a teaching assignment in Taiwan, and eventually graduate school at Yale University. Ultimately, I logged 10 years living in dormitories. Later in life, as landlord of one of the largest real estate holdings in the world, I discovered that I have a blind spot for people's attachment to their personal workspace. It never occurred to me that any perch would last very long.

With my MBA I set out to build a career, and my timing coincided with the massive productivity revolution across American industry. My corner of the automotive industry, Cummins Engine Company, was facing new and tough international competition and flipping old business models in response.

The transition was happening fast. To show how fast, I sat for examinations in 1980 to be professionally certified in inventory management. Within the year, however, the just-in-time resources management philosophy blew in and uprooted the entire field. I learned never to sit pretty on a skill base. It can vaporize in an instant.

Stage two of my career was varied as my husband and I moved to Boston and started a family. I worked in the professional services world as the CFO for an architecture firm, at an executive search firm, and at a diversity-consulting firm. The latter two equipped me for the surprise call from the Clinton-Gore Transition Team. I had skills to help the Presidential Personnel division respond to the President's instruction that his administration *look like America.* I signed on immediately.

From there I moved to the Department of Commerce as staff to Dave Barram, the Deputy Secretary, and then to GSA when he accepted the appointment as Administrator. As his

Chief of Staff, I supported him in aggressively introducing the use of the internet, choosing to offer real estate services competitively, and incorporating new legal mandates. We had a ball.

It was hard to leave vibrant government assignments, but I subsequently moved into consulting and then the information technology industry, where I often supported government clients. At one point, I held the title of Vice President–Culture and promoted creative strategies and skills for transforming large organizations. When I returned to GSA as Administrator, I had amassed experience in a surprising number of the agency's different business lines.

Every leader has a stash of formative stories. As a history major, I appreciate the value of a backstory in explaining motivation and passion. Leaders make a broad swath across an organization, and it is useful to understand what makes them tick. The key question when probing these stories is whether they harken back or lean forward. I am grateful that my stories yielded a string of lessons that repeatedly pushed me into the brave new world of creativity, risk, and change.

To engage with Martha Johnson in conversation about her leadership ideas, please visit www.MarthaJohnson.com.

32247401R00105

Made in the USA
Lexington, KY
13 May 2014